DOCTRINE & COVENANTS
COME FOLLOW ME ACTIVITY BOOK

2025

TWO ACTIVITY PAGES FOR EVERY WEEKLY COME FOLLOW ME LESSON FOR THE ENTIRE YEAR

THIS BOOK BELONGS TO:

_____

ABOUT THIS BOOK

This is an activity book for kids ages 6-11 that aligns with the weekly 2025 Come, Follow Me curriculum. Each week has two activity pages to complete. Enjoy!

© 2024 Latter-day Designs. All rights reserved.

This book is not made, approved, or endorsed by Intellectual Reserve, Inc. or The Church of Jesus Christ of Latter-day Saints.

MY GOALS FOR THIS YEAR

Write or draw your spiritual, physical, social, and intellectual goals for this year below.

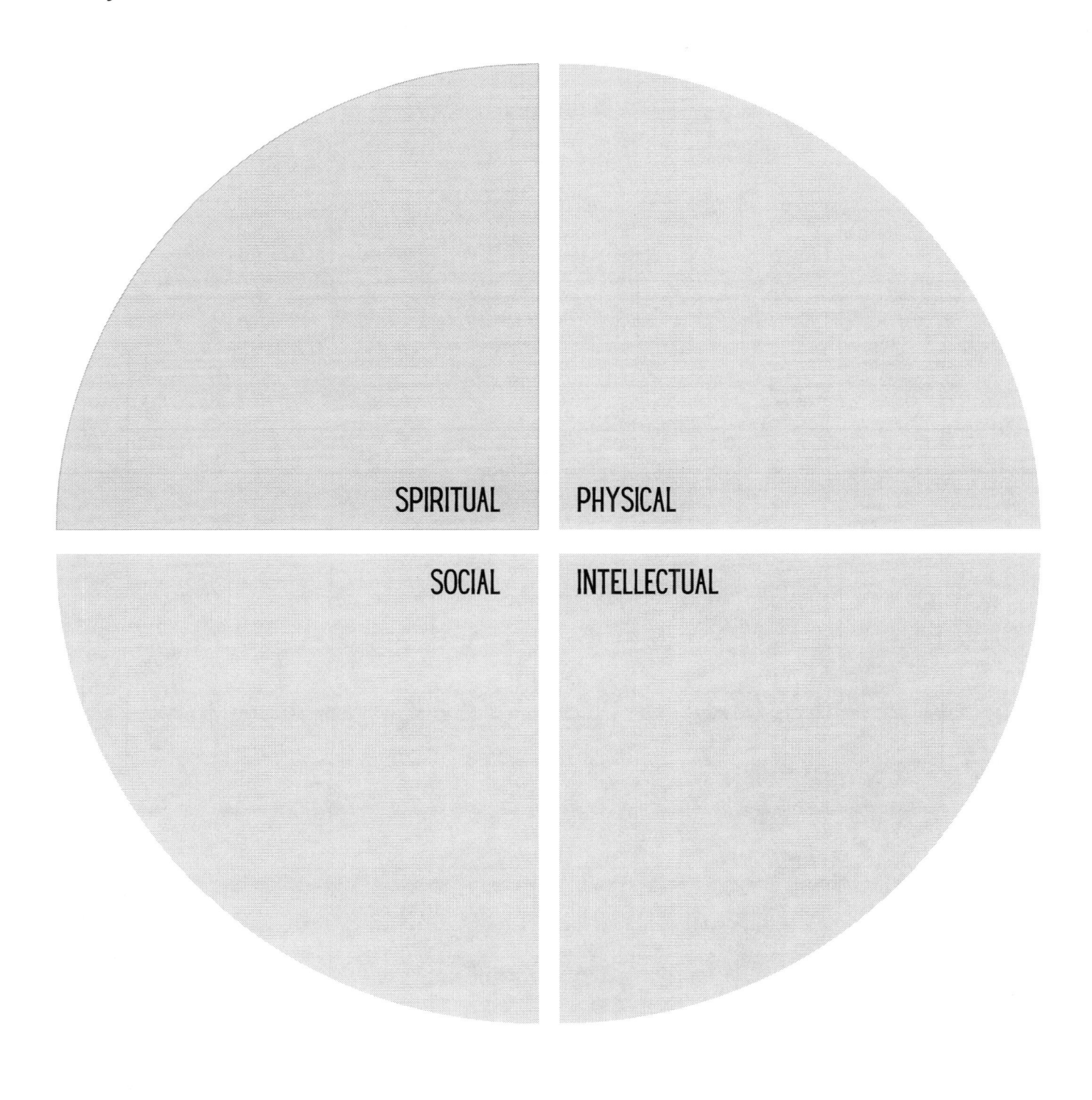

SPIRITUAL	PHYSICAL
SOCIAL	INTELLECTUAL

LESSON SCHEDULE

January
Dec 30-Jan 5	Restoration of the Gospel
Jan 6-12	D&C 1
Jan 13-19	JSH 1:1-26 & Voices of the Restoration: Joseph Smith's Family
Jan 20-26	D&C 2; JSH 1:27-65

February
Jan 27-Feb 2	D&C 3-5
Feb 3-9	D&C 6-9; Voices of the Restoration: Translation of the Book of Mormon
Feb 10-16	D&C 10-11
Feb 17-23	D&C 12-17; JSH 1:66-75; Voices of the Restoration: The Witnesses…

March
Feb 24-Mar 2	D&C 18
Mar 3-9	D&C 19
Mar 10-16	D&C 20-22
Mar 17-23	D&C 23-26; Voices of the Restoration: Emma Hale Smith
Mar 24-30	D&C 27-28

April
Mar 31-Apr 6	D&C 29
April 7-13	D&C 30-36; Voices of the Restoration: Early Converts
April 14-20	Easter
April 21-27	D&C 37-40; Voices of the Restoration: Gathering to Ohio

May
April 28-May 4	D&C 41-44
May 5-11	D&C 45
May 12-18	D&C 46-48
May 19-25	D&C 49-50

June
May 26-Jun 1	D&C 51-57
Jun 2-8	D&C 58-59
Jun 9-15	D&C 60-63
Jun 16-22	D&C 64-66
Jun 23-29	D&C 67-70

LESSON SCHEDULE

July
Jun 30-Jul 6	D&C 71-75
Jul 7-13	D&C 76; Voices of the Restoration: Testimonies of "the Vision"
Jul 14-20	D&C 77-80
Jul 21-27	D&C 81-83

August
Jul 28-Aug 3	D&C 84
Aug 4-10	D&C 85-87
Aug 11-17	D&C 88
Aug 18-24	D&C 89-92
Aug 25-31	D&C 93

September
Sept 1-7	D&C 94-97
Sept 8-14	D&C 98-101
Sept 15-21	D&C 102-105; Voices of the Restoration: Zion's Camp
Sept 22-28	D&C 106-108

October
Sept 29-Oct 5	D&C 109-110; Voices of the Restoration: …and the Kirtland Temple
Oct 6-12	D&C 111-114
Oct 13-19	D&C 115-120
Oct 20-26	D&C 121-123; Voices of the Restoration: Liberty Jail

November
Oct 27-Nov 2	D&C 124; Voices of the Restoration: The Relief Society
Nov 3-9	D&C 125-128; Voices of the Restoration: Baptism for our Ancestors
Nov 10-16	D&C 129-132
Nov 17-23	D&C 133-134
Nov 24-30	D&C 135-136

December
Dec 1-7	D&C 137-138
Dec 8-14	Articles of Faith and Official Declarations 1 & 2
Dec 15-21	The Family: A Proclamation to the World
Dec 22-28	Christmas

DECEMBER 30 - JANUARY 5

CIRCLE THE DAYS YOU READ THIS WEEK: MON TUES WED THUR FRI SAT SUN

Heavenly Father chose Joseph Smith as His prophet to help restore the Savior's gospel. In the Doctrine and Covenants and Joseph Smith History (JSH), we learn about six angels that helped restore the gospel. Read D&C 27:12, D&C 110:13-16, JSH 1:33, 72 with your family or primary class to find the names of the six angels who visited Joseph. Color the angel wings below that list the names of these heavenly messengers.

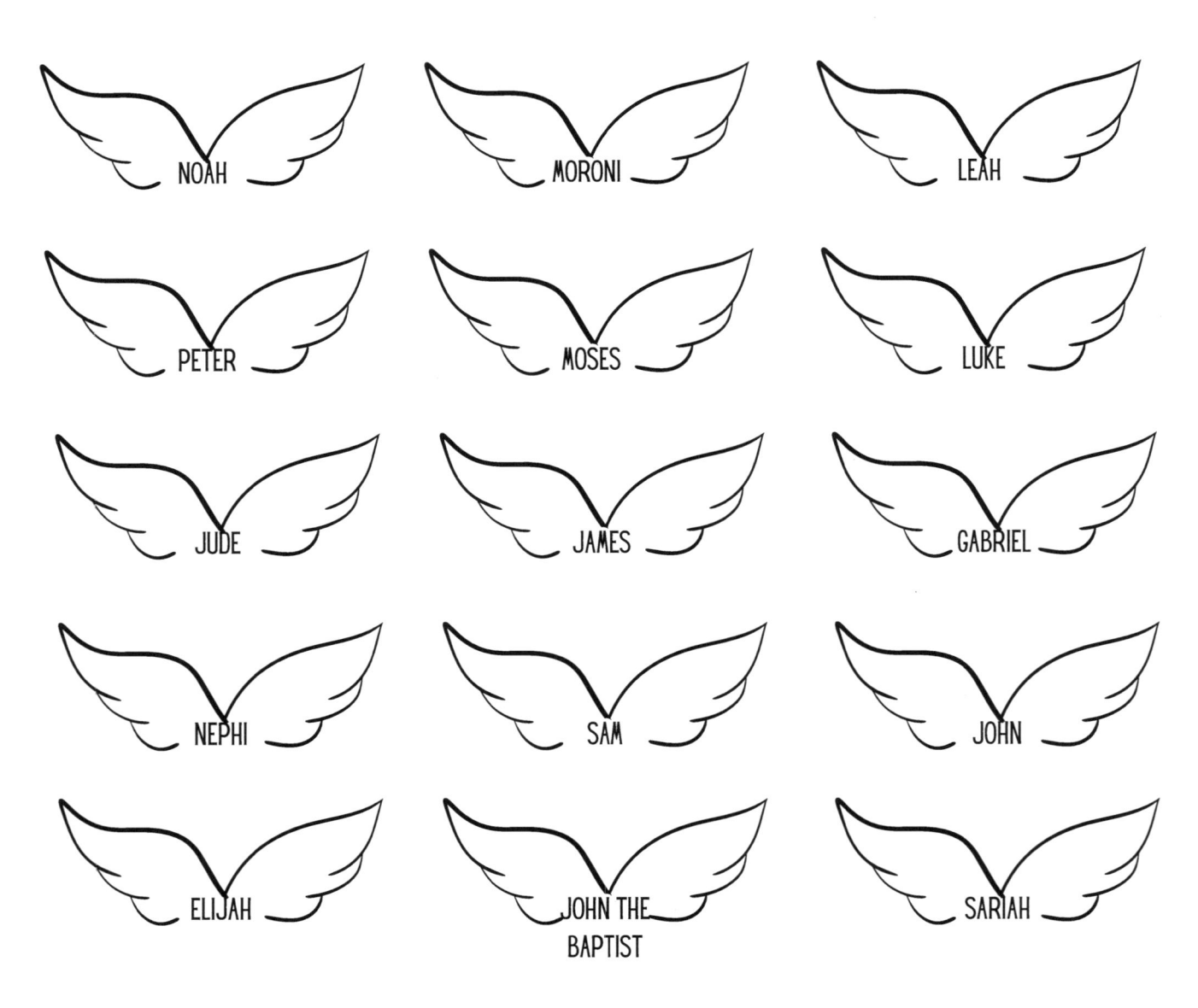

NOAH	MORONI	LEAH
PETER	MOSES	LUKE
JUDE	JAMES	GABRIEL
NEPHI	SAM	JOHN
ELIJAH	JOHN THE BAPTIST	SARIAH

ANGELS CAME TO INSTRUCT JOSEPH

RESTORATION OF THE GOSPEL

As you study the Doctrine & Covenants this year, it is first important to learn the history of how the Restoration of Christ's gospel began. Match each statement below to the correct picture. Color the pictures.

JOSEPH WENT TO THE HILL CUMORAH TO SEE THE PLATES. AFTER FOUR YEARS, HE WAS ABLE TO TAKE THE PLATES & BEGIN TRANSLATING THE BOOK OF MORMON.

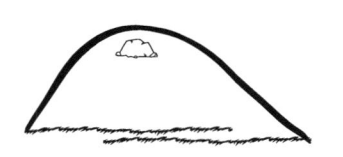

AT AGE 14, JOSEPH SMITH WENT TO THE WOODS TO PRAY. HEAVENLY FATHER & JESUS APPEARED TO HIM & TOLD HIM TO JOIN NONE OF THE CHURCHES.

JOSEPH SMITH HAD QUESTIONS TO ASK GOD. HE DIDN'T KNOW WHICH CHURCH TO JOIN.

AT AGE 17, THE ANGEL MORONI CAME & TOLD JOSEPH ABOUT A BOOK WRITTEN ON GOLD PLATES BUIRED NEAR HIS HOME.

JANUARY 6-12

CIRCLE THE DAYS YOU READ THIS WEEK: MON TUES WED THUR FRI SAT SUN

Can you think of warning signs you have seen? We see road signs that let us know about curves ahead so we know to slow down. After mopping a floor, janitors often put out signs to let us know the floor is slippery. Prophets also give us warnings from the Lord. On the signs below, write some warnings the prophets have given to us. For example, you may write something like "don't forget to pray daily" on one of the signs.

THE LORD WARNS US OF SPIRITUAL DANGERS THROUGH HIS PROPHETS

D&C 1

The Lord called Joseph Smith to be a prophet. Read D&C 1:17 & 29. How do you know that the Lord called upon Joseph to be His servant? Color the picture below of the prophet Joseph.

THE LORD CALLED JOSEPH SMITH TO BE A PROPHET

JANUARY 13-19

CIRCLE THE DAYS YOU READ THIS WEEK: MON TUES WED THUR FRI SAT SUN

Joseph Smith was born December 23, 1805 in Vermont to Joseph Smith, Sr. and Lucy Mack Smith. They were good parents who loved God. Joseph had five brothers & three sisters. Draw faces on Joseph's family below and color.

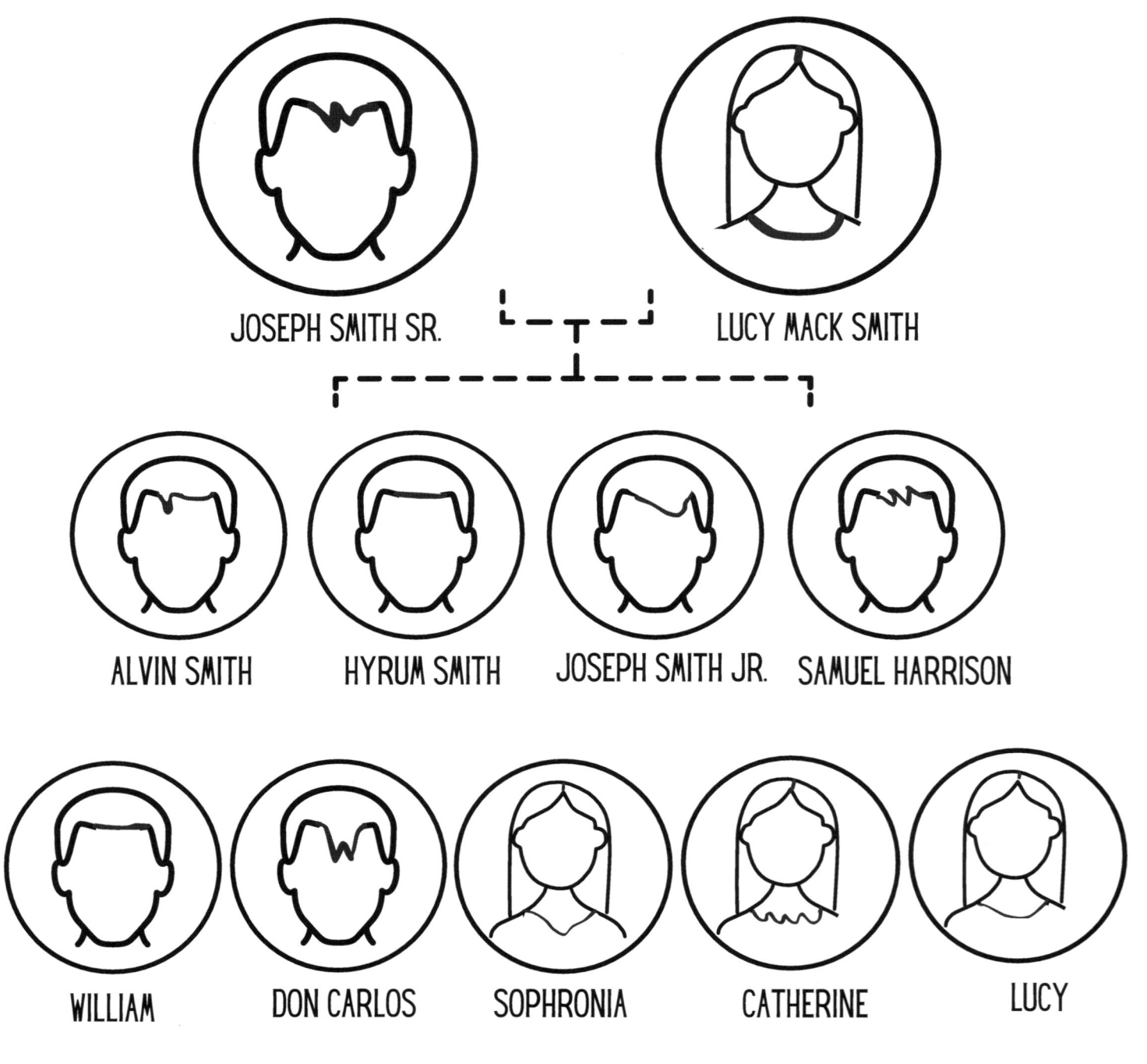

JOSEPH SMITH SR. LUCY MACK SMITH

ALVIN SMITH HYRUM SMITH JOSEPH SMITH JR. SAMUEL HARRISON

WILLIAM DON CARLOS SOPHRONIA CATHERINE LUCY

JOSEPH SMITH WAS PREPARED TO BE A PROPHET

JSH 1:1-26 &
VOICES OF THE RESTORATON: JOSEPH SMITH'S FAMILY

Joseph had questions about religion and which church he should join. Joseph turned to the Bible to find answers. In the blank thought bubble below, write a gospel question you have. Search for the answer in the scriptures with your family.

HOW SHALL I KNOW WHICH CHURCH IS RIGHT?

As Joseph Smith was reading James 1:5, he felt he should follow the scripture's advice and ask God his questions. Fill in the missing words from James 1:5 below.

IF ANY OF YOU LACK _____, LET HIM _____ OF GOD, THAT _____ TO ALL MEN _____, AND UPBRAIDETH NOT; AND IT _____ BE GIVEN HIM.

JAMES 1:5

ASK   LIBERALLY   WISDOM   GIVETH   SHALL

GOD CAN ANSWER MY QUESTIONS THROUGH THE SCRIPTURES

JANUARY 20-26

CIRCLE THE DAYS YOU READ THIS WEEK: MON TUES WED THUR FRI SAT SUN

Angel Moroni visited Joseph and told him about golden plates buried near his home. Joseph went to the Hill Cumorah and saw the plates but was not able to take them home until four years later. In the maze below, find the right entrance to get to the Hill Cumorah.

PICK THE RIGHT PATH TO FIND THE HILL CUMORAH

GOD PREPARED THE PROPHET JOSEPH TO HELP HIM WITH HIS WORK

D&C 2; JSH 1:27-65

In D&C 2, we learn about the mission of Elijah, which is to turn the hearts of the children to their fathers. One way we can do this is through learning about our ancestors. Ask your family to share some stories with you about your ancestors. Fill out the family tree below and write the names of you and your family below.

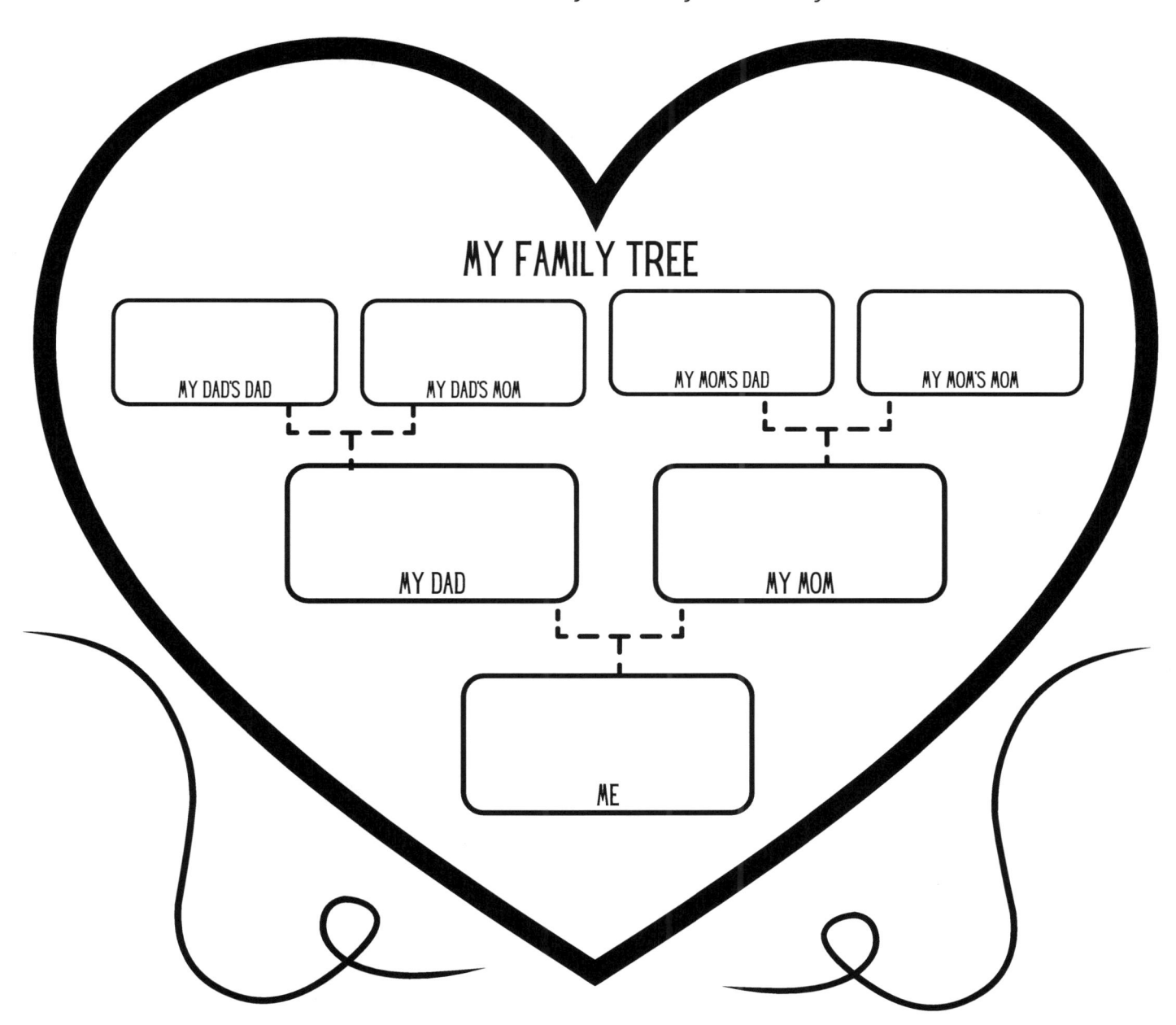

MY FAMILY TREE

| MY DAD'S DAD | MY DAD'S MOM | MY MOM'S DAD | MY MOM'S MOM |

| MY DAD | MY MOM |

ME

I CAN FEEL JOY BY LEARNING ABOUT MY ANCESTORS

JANUARY 27-FEBRUARY 2

CIRCLE THE DAYS YOU READ THIS WEEK: MON TUES WED THUR FRI SAT SUN

In D&C section 4, the Lord gives us an invitation. Crack the code below to see what the invitation is.

CRACK THE CODE

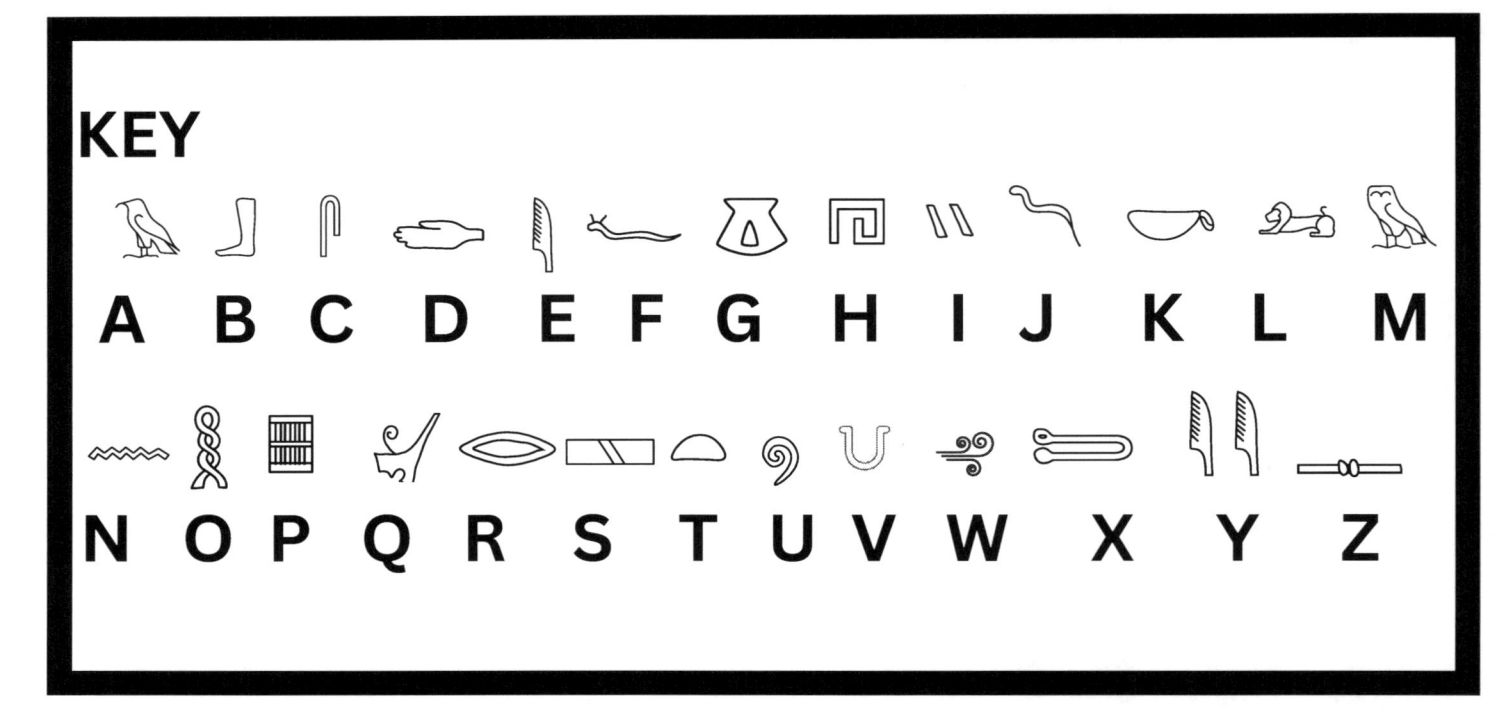

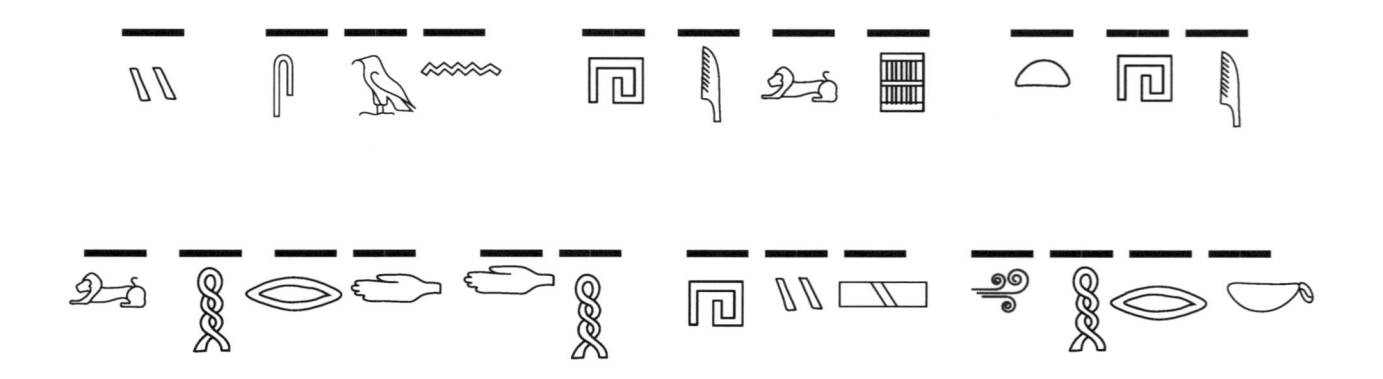

___ ___ ___ ___ ___   ___ ___ ___ ___ ___ ___ ___

___ ___ ___ ___ ___ ___ ___ ___ ___ ___ ___ ___ ___ ___

D&C 3-5

Joseph gave his friend Martin Harris 116 pages of the translation of the Book of Mormon to show to his wife. The pages were lost and Joseph and Martin were chastised by the Lord. What do you learn from this account about trusting God and not giving into peer pressure? Complete the word search below.

```
W  O  U  V  F  A  I  V  C  X  G  W  F  B  O
B  P  Y  O  L  F  C  J  X  Z  P  Y  X  F  V
Z  Q  N  A  P  O  D  J  E  G  A  D  C  N  R
I  V  D  E  T  B  T  U  J  A  G  V  Z  P  R
J  G  V  V  G  N  M  F  T  N  E  X  Z  R  K
P  R  I  I  N  D  E  S  I  T  S  A  H  C  C
L  W  K  G  C  I  U  P  L  A  U  T  P  L  W
S  H  X  R  D  R  W  H  E  V  R  U  B  G  O
H  Y  J  O  T  W  M  E  H  R  I  O  U  D  Q
A  F  J  F  L  S  U  K  M  I  W  O  Z  C  C
U  Q  P  M  Z  T  O  Q  A  C  Q  X  D  J  M
R  V  X  M  O  X  C  L  L  H  W  R  J  H  V
N  Q  E  G  F  Y  O  D  T  I  V  O  H  A  K
Z  F  D  A  M  R  H  P  E  S  O  J  U  I  N
I  N  D  Y  D  E  M  K  Z  M  A  R  T  I  N
```

JOSEPH	MARTIN	PAGES
LOST	LORD	CHASTISED
REPENT	TRUST	FORGIVE

I CAN CHOOSE THE RIGHT EVEN WHEN OTHERS TRY TO GET ME TO CHOOSE WRONG

FEBRUARY 3-9

CIRCLE THE DAYS YOU READ THIS WEEK: MON TUES WED THUR FRI SAT SUN

In D&C 6:34, the Lord tells Joseph and Oliver Cowdery to not fear but to look to Him with faith. Find the hidden pictures amongst the sheep below.

"FEAR NOT, LITTLE FLOCK"

D&C 6-9; VOICES OF THE RESTORATION: TRANSLATION OF THE BOOK OF MORMON

Complete the cross-word puzzle below with words that relate to this week's reading.

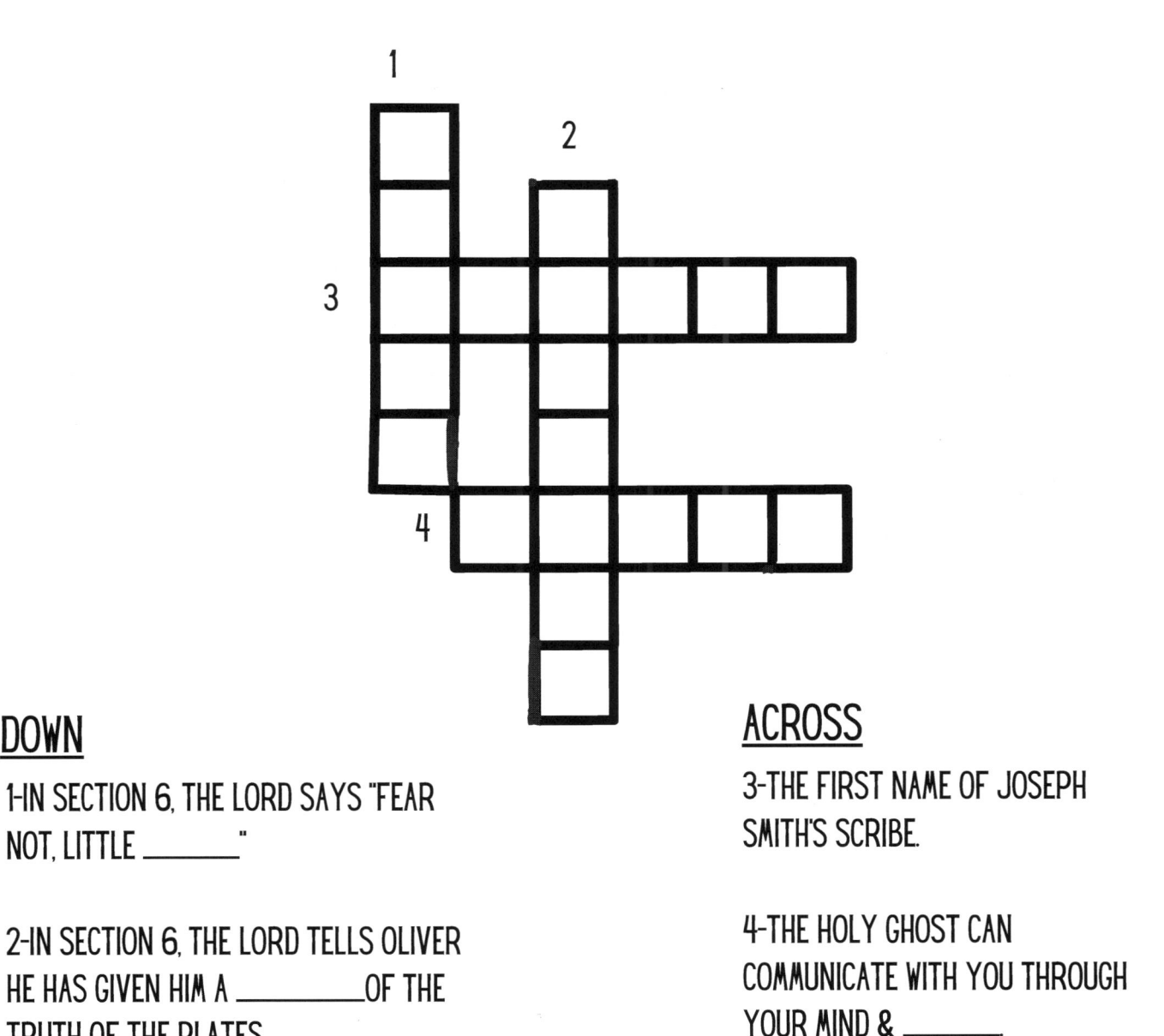

DOWN

1- IN SECTION 6, THE LORD SAYS "FEAR NOT, LITTLE _____"

2- IN SECTION 6, THE LORD TELLS OLIVER HE HAS GIVEN HIM A _____ OF THE TRUTH OF THE PLATES.

ACROSS

3- THE FIRST NAME OF JOSEPH SMITH'S SCRIBE.

4- THE HOLY GHOST CAN COMMUNICATE WITH YOU THROUGH YOUR MIND & _____

I CAN LOOK TO JESUS IN EVERY THOUGHT

FEBRUARY 10-16

CIRCLE THE DAYS YOU READ THIS WEEK: MON TUES WED THUR FRI SAT SUN

In D&C 10:5, it tells us we should "pray always". Color the words below that rhyme with "pray".

RHYME TIME: FIND WORDS THAT RHYME WITH "PRAY"

STRAY	PARTY	PAY	PRINT	HURRAY
FLY	MEDITATE	THINK	ALWAYS	SWAY
MAY	POOR	PRANCE	SPRAY	AWAY
FRAY	PREY	READ	STAY	PIE

I CAN PRAY ALWAYS

D&C 10-11

In D&C 11:12-13, we are told the Holy Ghost "enlightens" our minds and fills our souls "with joy". Find the correct number of objects that produce light below. Color each item as you go.

☆ 11   🕯 7   ☀ 4   🪔 5   🔥 3   🔦 5   🌙 6

THE HOLY GHOST LEADS ME TO DO GOOD

FEBRUARY 17-23

CIRCLE THE DAYS YOU READ THIS WEEK: MON TUES WED THUR FRI SAT SUN

In D&C 17, the Lord teaches that He uses witnesses to establish His word. Think about ways you can be a witness of the Book of Mormon. Use the letters in the words "I can be a witness" to see how many words you can make.

I CAN BE A WITNESS

Book of Mormon

D&C 12-17; JSH 1:66-75; VOICES OF THE RESTORATION: THE WITNESSES OF THE BOOK OF MORMON

In D&C 13 and Joseph Smith—History 1:68–74, we read that John the Baptist gives the Aaronic Priesthood to Joseph Smith and Oliver Cowdery. After, Joseph and Oliver went and baptized each other. Draw a picture of one of these two events below.

JOHN THE BAPTIST RESTORED THE AARONIC PRIESTHOOD

FEBRUARY 24–MARCH 2

CIRCLE THE DAYS YOU READ THIS WEEK: MON TUES WED THUR FRI SAT SUN

In D&C 18:10–13, we are told that all of us are important and of great worth to God. How do you treat something that is valuable to you? Knowing that others are valuable to God, how should we treat others? Draw a picture of yourself in the frame below.

YOU ARE OF GREAT WORTH TO GOD

D&C 18

In D&C 18:13–16, we read that sharing the gospel with others and bringing them to Christ brings us joy. Color the picture of the missionaries below. Write ways you can or have shared the gospel in the ovals below.

SHARING THE GOSPEL BRINGS ME JOY

MARCH 3-9

CIRCLE THE DAYS YOU READ THIS WEEK: MON TUES WED THUR FRI SAT SUN

In D&C 19:16-19, Jesus tells us that He suffered for us so we can repent of our sins. Complete the word search below with words related to this scripture passage.

```
W P V U H K A H O C G T P E G
M A A W Z Y B S U F F E R E D
S S Z O O W J L F H K J P K R
D A V F I Z T H Y J W I W K Z
K Z C T A T O N E M E N T C N
F L N R Q M O F Y Y B S M G M
O B G K A J J P M B N X U Y M
P B R X I M Q F Y V M G W S W
H U A S A N E G I Z P P Q Q X
O L L O R I D N Z H L Q M Q F
X O S V B W O N T O P X F X W
D V K E S T Z F E S A R J K Z
R E P E N T N Á A S L S A F C
P W F U N Z N S I N S L H Y C
L Y Z Y X Q X T M O L X F C N
```

JESUS	SUFFERED	SINS
ATONEMENT	REPENT	LOVE
PRAY	KINDNESS	SACRAMENT

BECAUSE JESUS SUFFRED FOR ME, I CAN REPENT

D&C 19

In D&C 19:26–41, we read about the sacrifice Martin Harris made in having to sell a large portion of his farm to pay the printer for the copies of the Book of Mormon. What sacrifices does the Lord ask you to make? The Lord tells us that His blessings are greater than the treasures of the earth. Color the treasure box and list some of the blessings God gives you on the coins.

GOD'S BLESSINGS ARE GREATER THAN THE TREASURES OF THE EARTH

MARCH 10-16

CIRCLE THE DAYS YOU READ THIS WEEK: MON TUES WED THUR FRI SAT SUN

On April 6, 1830, the Lord's Church was restored to the earth. See D&C 20-21 for further study with your family or primary class. Find six differences between the two churches below and circle them on the bottom picture.

SPOT THE DIFFERENCES

THE LORD'S CHURCH WAS RESTORED

D&C 20-22

In D&C 20:37, 41, 71–74, we learn about being baptized and receiving the gift of the Holy Ghost. Color the picture of the boy being baptized below.

BAPTISMAL COVENANTS

I PROMISE TO:
- TAKE CHRIST'S NAME UPON ME
- SERVE THE LORD & OTHERS
- OBEY COMMANDMENTS

HEAVENLY FATHER PROMISES TO:
- FORGIVE ME WHEN I MAKE MISTAKES
- GIVE ME THE COMPANIONSHIP OF THE HOLY GHOST
- MAKE IT POSSIBLE FOR ME TO LIVE WITH HIM AGAIN

HOW DO YOU RENEW YOUR BAPTISMAL COVENANTS EACH WEEK?

MARCH 17-23

CIRCLE THE DAYS YOU READ THIS WEEK: MON TUES WED THUR FRI SAT SUN

In D&C 25, the Lord gives Emma counsel on what he would like her to do. Color the picture of Emma and some of the things she was asked to do by the Lord below.

CREATE FIRST HYMN BOOK OF CHURCH

ASSIST IN TRANSLATING THE BOOK OF MORMON AS A SCRIBE, FOR A TIME

COMFORT THE PROPHET JOSEPH IN HIS AFFLICTIONS

EMMA HALE SMITH WAS AN ELECT LADY

D&C 23-26;
VOICES OF THE RESTORATION: EMMA HALE SMITH

In D&C 25:13, we are told to "cleave" unto our covenants. Cleave means to hold onto something firmly. Just like we can glue two pieces of paper together, we can think of gluing our covenants to our hearts so as not to forget them. Below, color the glue bottles that have synonyms (words that mean something similar) to the word "cleave".

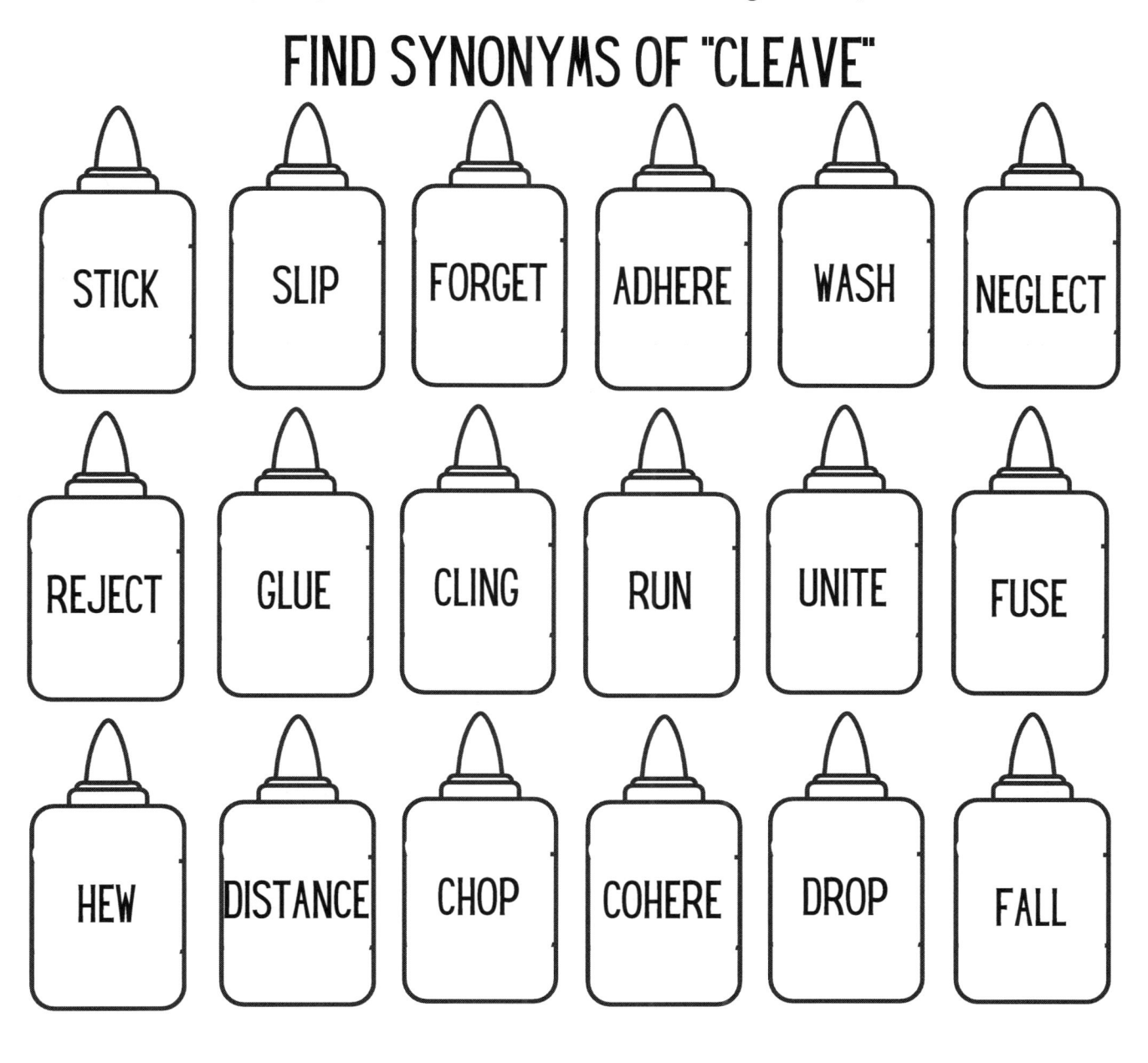

FIND SYNONYMS OF "CLEAVE"

- STICK
- SLIP
- FORGET
- ADHERE
- WASH
- NEGLECT
- REJECT
- GLUE
- CLING
- RUN
- UNITE
- FUSE
- HEW
- DISTANCE
- CHOP
- COHERE
- DROP
- FALL

MY COVENANTS BRING ME JOY

MARCH 24-30

CIRCLE THE DAYS YOU READ THIS WEEK: MON TUES WED THUR FRI SAT SUN

In D&C 27, we learn about how the armor of God protects us. On the armor below, fill in the missing word for each piece of armor that describes how it spiritually protects us. Use D&C 27 to help you find the missing words.

THE HELMET OF _____

THE SHIELD OF _____

THE SWORD OF MY _____

THE BREASTPLATE OF _____

LOINS GIRT ABOUT WITH _____

FEET SHOD WITH PREPARATION OF THE GOSPEL OF _____

THE ARMOR OF GOD PROTECTS ME

D&C 27-28

In D&C 27:1-4, we learn why we now use water instead of wine for our sacrament services. Also, we are taught that the sacrament helps us remember Jesus. In the maze below, make your way from the bread and water to Jesus.

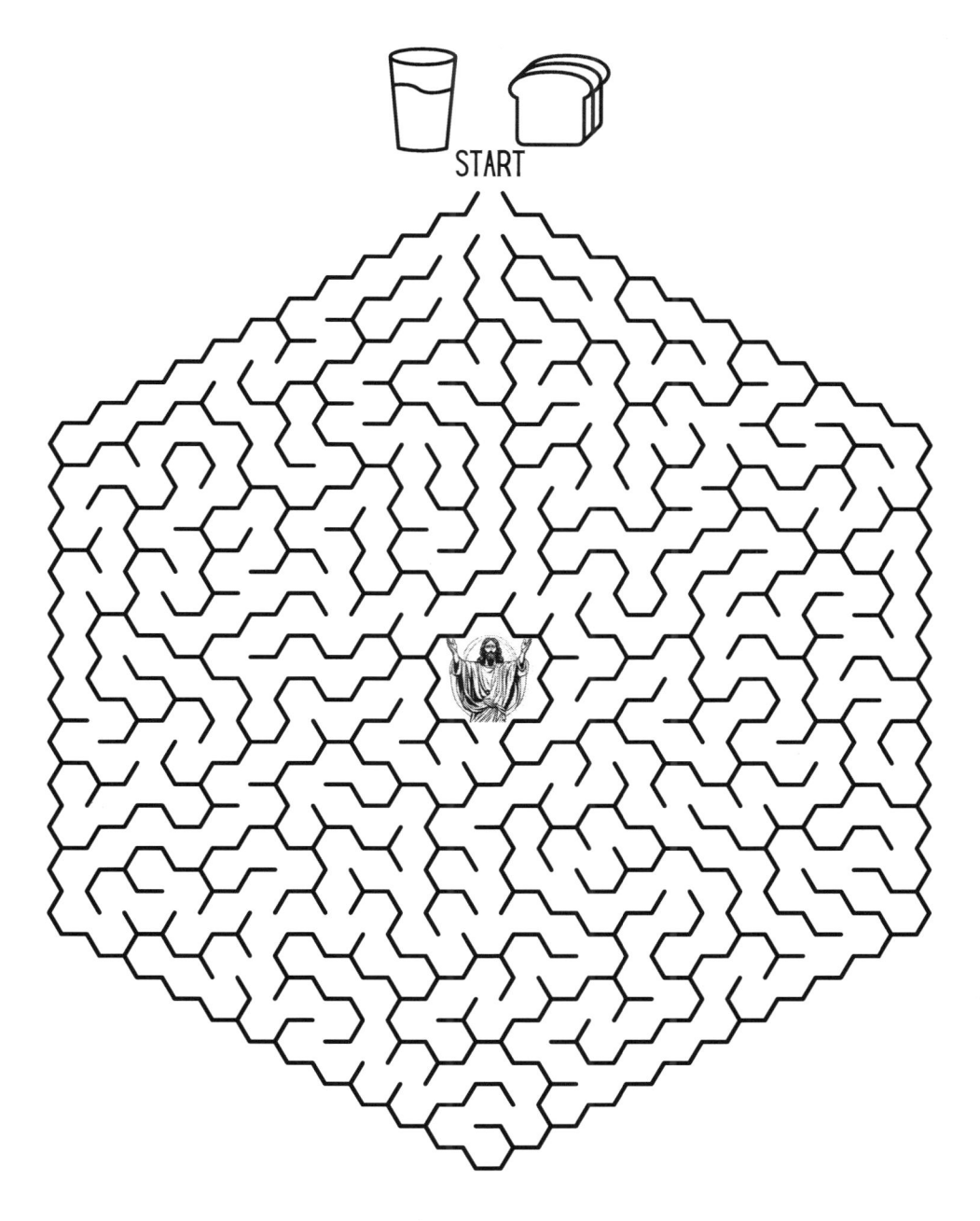

START

THE SACRAMENT HELPS ME REMEMBER JESUS

MARCH 31-APRIL 6

CIRCLE THE DAYS YOU READ THIS WEEK: MON TUES WED THUR FRI SAT SUN

In D&C 29:1-2 and 7-8, we read how the Lord is gathering His people like a hen gathers her chicks. Write on the chicks how you can help with missionary work and with the "gathering" before the second coming and then color the picture.

I CAN HELP GATHER HIS PEOPLE BEFORE HE COMES AGAIN

D&C 29

In D&C 29:11, Jesus tells us He will come again. Fill in the missing words for this scripture verse below and see if you can memorize it!

FOR I WILL REVEAL MYSELF FROM _____ WITH _____ AND GREAT _____, WITH ALL THE HOSTS THEREOF, AND DWELL IN _____ WITH MEN ON EARTH A _____ YEARS, AND THE _____ SHALL NOT STAND.
-D&C 29:11

WICKED   RIGHTEOUSNESS   POWER   HEAVEN   THOUSAND   GLORY

WRITE WAYS YOU CAN FOLLOW IN CHRIST'S FOOTSTEPS & PREPARE FOR HIM COMING AGAIN IN FOOTPRINTS BELOW:

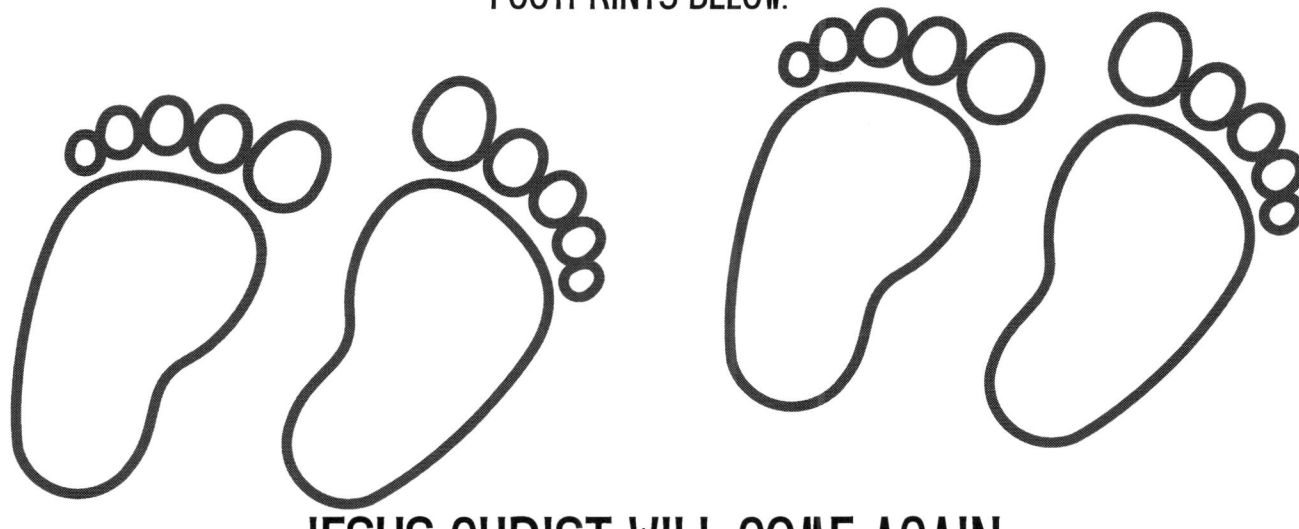

JESUS CHRIST WILL COME AGAIN

APRIL 7-13

CIRCLE THE DAYS YOU READ THIS WEEK: MON TUES WED THUR FRI SAT SUN

In D&C 33:8-10, the Lord gives us advice on sharing the gospel with others. Crack the code below to find out what that message is. Discuss with your family or primary class what you think the message means.

CRACK THE CODE

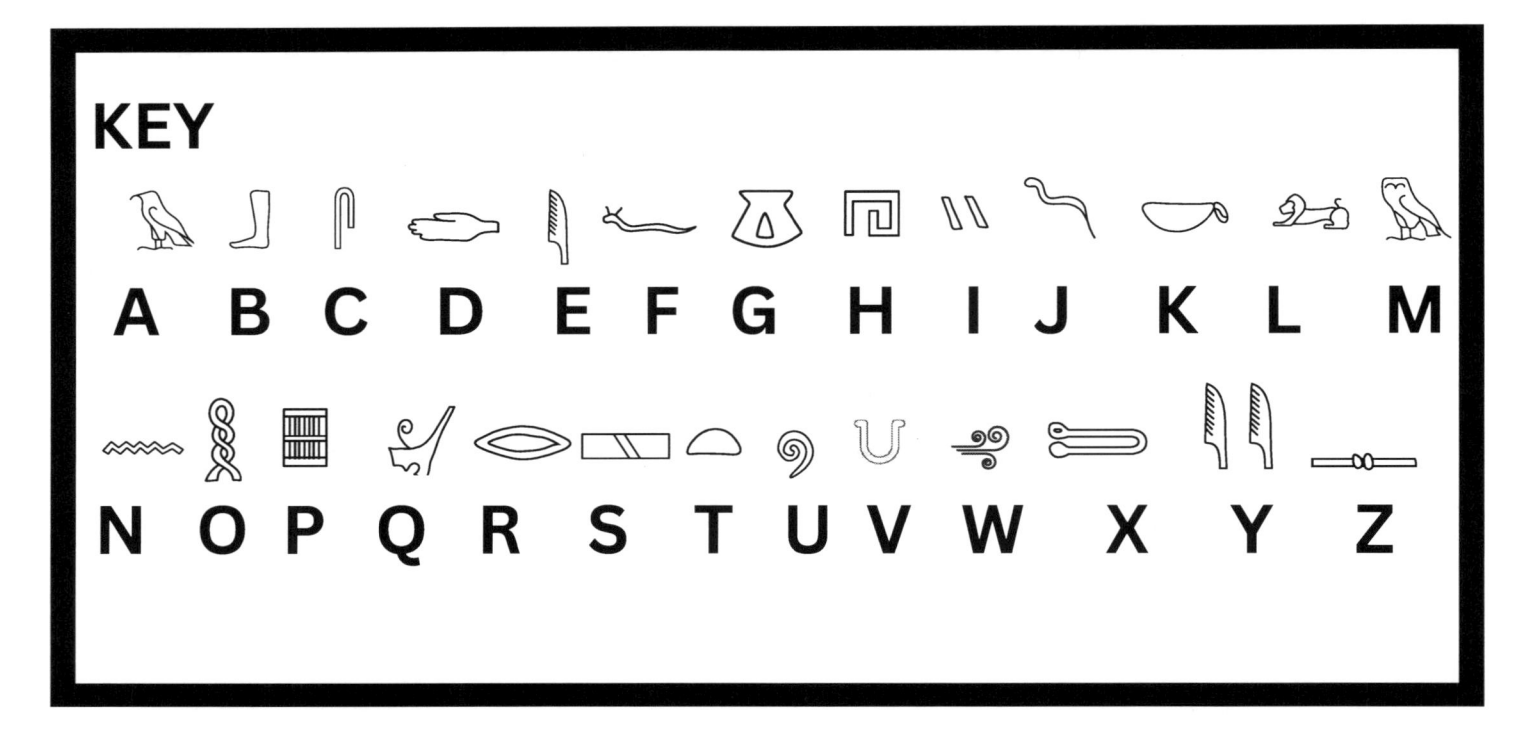

KEY

A B C D E F G H I J K L M
N O P Q R S T U V W X Y Z

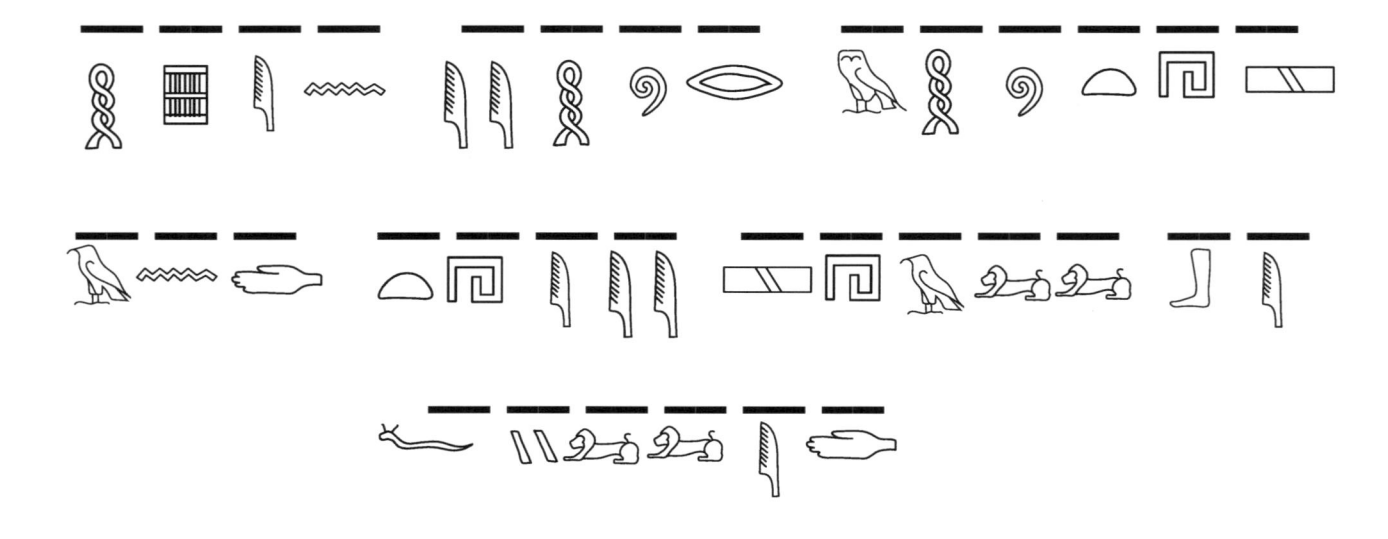

_ _ _ _ _   _ _ _ _   _ _ _ _ _ _ _

_ _ _ _ _   _ _ _ _ _ _   _ _ _ _ _

_ _ _ _ _ _ _

D&C 30-36;
VOICES OF THE RESTORATION: EARLY CONVERTS

In D&C 33:2-3, we are told the Lord wants us to share the gospel with others. How can you prepare to be a full-time missionary someday? Where do you think you may be called to serve? Write your name on the name tag below and color the pictures.

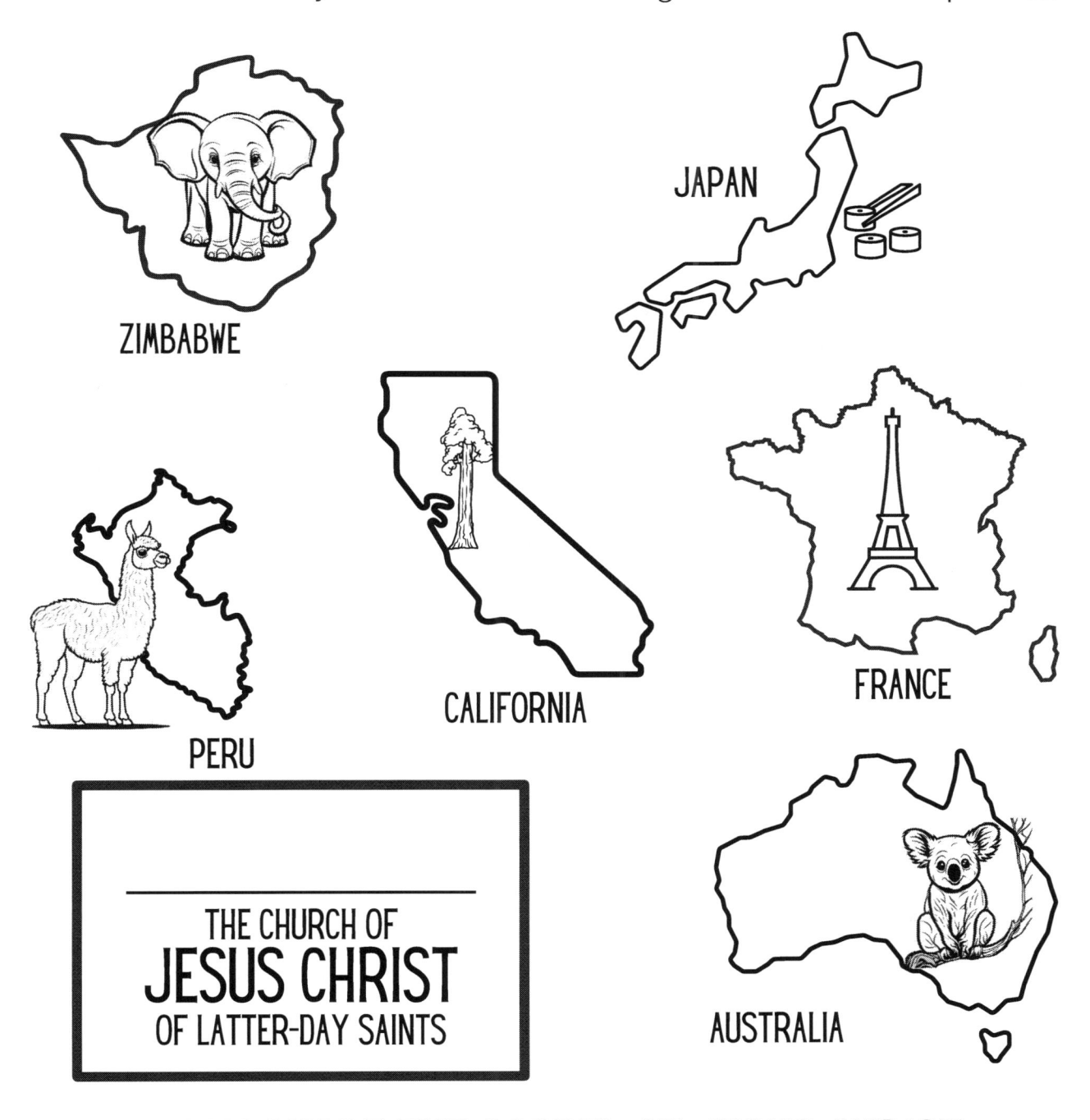

ZIMBABWE

JAPAN

PERU

CALIFORNIA

FRANCE

THE CHURCH OF
JESUS CHRIST
OF LATTER-DAY SAINTS

AUSTRALIA

I CAN SHARE THE GOSPEL OF JESUS CHRIST

APRIL 14-20

CIRCLE THE DAYS YOU READ THIS WEEK: MON TUES WED THUR FRI SAT SUN

Put the events of Holy Week in order below, by numbering the first event with a "1" and the second event with a "2" and so forth. Ask your family or primary class for assistance, if needed. You can also reference Matthew chapters 21-28.

#___
RESURRECTED JESUS APPEARS TO MARY MAGDALENE

#___
JESUS SUFFERS FOR OUR SINS IN GARDEN OF GETHSEMANE

#___
JESUS TEACHES THE PEOPLE PARABLES

#___
JESUS IS RESURRECTED & BODY THEN PLACED IN A TOMB

#___
JESUS' TRIUMPHAL ENTRY INTO JERUSALEM ON A DONKEY & PEOPLE WAVING PALM BRANCHES

#___
JESUS INTRODUCED THE ORDINANCE OF THE SACRAMENT TO HIS APOSTLES AT THE LAST SUPPER

EASTER

In D&C 138:17, it tells us that our bodies will be reunited with our spirits at the resurrection. Help the spirit pick the right path below to be reunited with it's body.

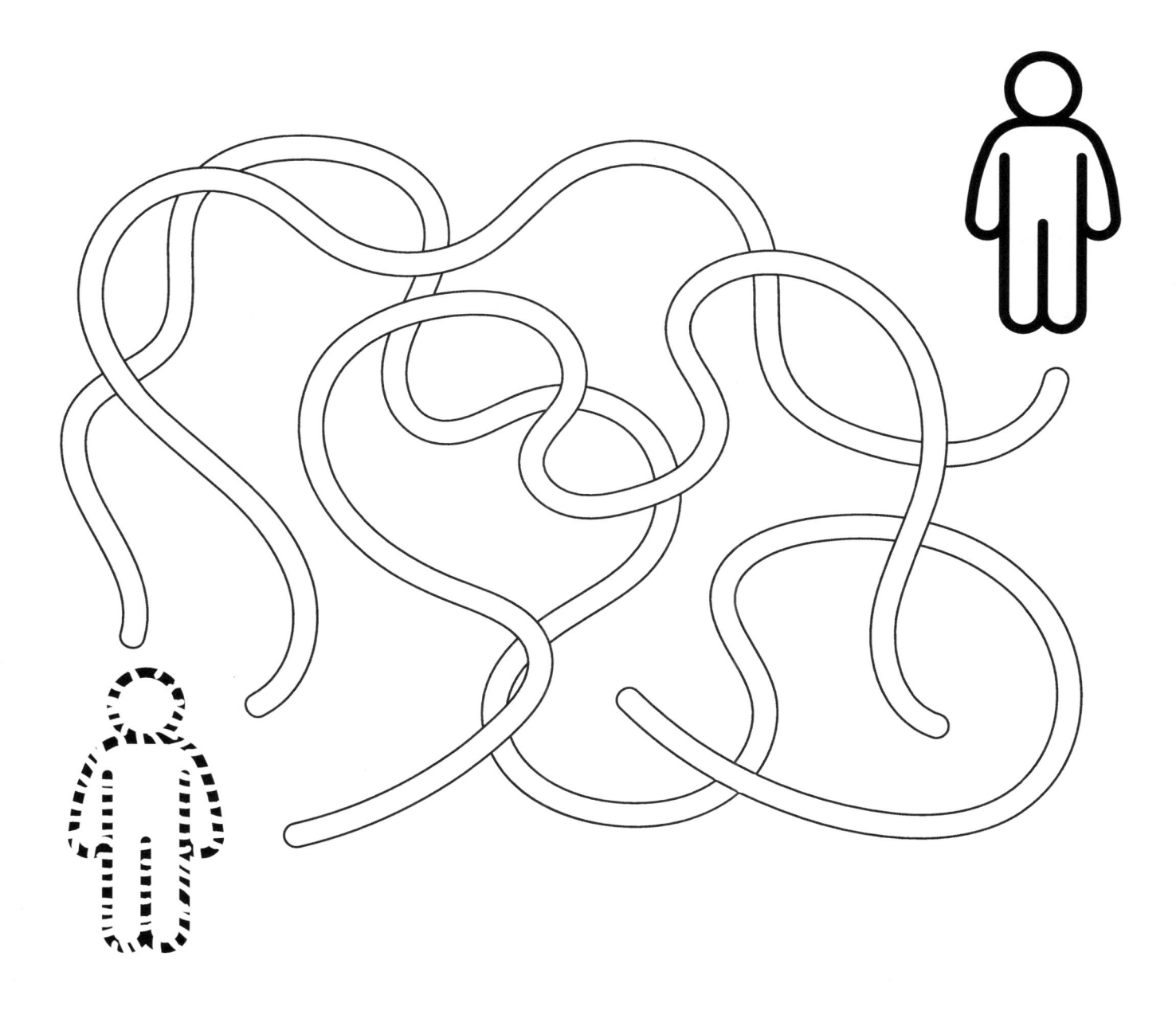

BECAUSE OF JESUS, I WILL BE RESURRECTED

APRIL 21-27

CIRCLE THE DAYS YOU READ THIS WEEK: MON TUES WED THUR FRI SAT SUN

In D&C 37-38, we read about members of the Church having to make sacrifices to gather in Ohio. They didn't have cars and planes back then, so it was a big effort to move that far away. Why do you think the Lord likes to gather His people? Circle the **10 items** below that you would take with you if you were one of these early saints moving to Ohio.

THE LORD GATHERS US TO BLESS US

D&C 37-40;
VOICES OF THE RESTORATION: GATHERING TO OHIO

In D&C 38:24-27, the Lord teaches us we should "be one". A quilt has unique and individual patches, but comes together as one blanket when sewn together. Likewise, we can unite as "one" as God's people despite being different, unique individuals. Color the quilt below.

GOD WANTS US TO BE ONE

APRIL 28-MAY 4

CIRCLE THE DAYS YOU READ THIS WEEK: MON TUES WED THUR FRI SAT SUN

Complete the word search below with words related to this week's reading. Topics include being a disciple, finding happiness by obeying commandments, sharing with the poor, and only the prophet receiving revelation for the whole Church.

```
Q  P  H  E  A  R  K  E  N  B  O  O  W  M  T
W  J  O  J  P  J  J  G  B  H  Q  S  P  T  Q
C  X  V  O  X  Q  T  V  N  B  O  X  R  V  U
C  K  C  H  R  E  V  E  L  A  T  I  O  N  D
C  O  N  S  E  C  R  A  T  I  O  N  P  R  I
X  H  B  W  R  A  T  W  H  E  V  N  H  N  S
T  A  O  P  Q  P  R  I  T  Y  B  E  E  C
K  F  F  Q  E  R  P  N  O  J  F  N  T  L  I
B  R  D  G  E  G  F  J  M  I  T  S  F  S  P
S  O  B  E  Y  S  Z  E  U  S  K  L  F  F  L
B  E  E  P  P  X  Y  G  Q  T  H  Y  O  N  E
X  W  R  Q  H  B  N  W  Y  F  S  J  W  Q  B
H  B  L  V  M  T  O  Q  P  N  U  M  Z  V  R
O  M  B  Z  E  N  T  H  P  X  H  Q  Q  J  X
V  U  G  J  A  G  R  L  H  T  V  D  J  K  V
```

DISCIPLE	OBEYS	HEAR
HEARKEN	SERVE	PROPHET
REVELATION	CONSECRATION	POOR

D&C 41-44

CIRCLE THE DAYS YOU READ THIS WEEK: MON TUES WED THUR FRI SAT SUN

In D&C 42:30-42, we learn that we are to share with the poor. One way you help serve those in need is to fast once per month for two meals and give the money you would have spent on those two meals as a fast offering. The Church then uses that money to help those in need. Draw two meals on the plates below and calculate how much each of those meals would cost. Color the pictures below.

HOW MUCH WOULD THESE TWO MEALS COST? _____

FAST OFFERINGS GIVE FOOD, CLOTHING, AND NECESSITIES TO THOSE WHO ARE POOR AND NEEDY.

CHRIST WANTS ME TO HELP THE POOR

MAY 5-11

CIRCLE THE DAYS YOU READ THIS WEEK: MON TUES WED THUR FRI SAT SUN

In D&C 45:32, we are told to "stand in holy places". Where are some of the holy places you can go?

I CAN STAND IN HOLY PLACES

D&C 45

CIRCLE THE DAYS YOU READ THIS WEEK: MON TUES WED THUR FRI SAT SUN

Read the following scripture verses in D&C 45 that teach about the Second Coming. Match each scripture passage to the corresponding image. This would be a great activity to do with your family or primary class.

D&C 45:44-45

D&C 45:51-52

D&C 45:55

D&C 45:58-59

D&C 45:66-71

JESUS WILL COME AGAIN

MAY 12-18

CIRCLE THE DAYS YOU READ THIS WEEK: MON TUES WED THUR FRI SAT SUN

In D&C 46:13-26, we learn that the Lord has given each of us spiritual gifts to bless the lives of those around us. In the boxes below, color gifts you think you have. In the blank gift boxes, write a gift you have that is not listed. If you are unsure, talk with your family about gifts they think you have.

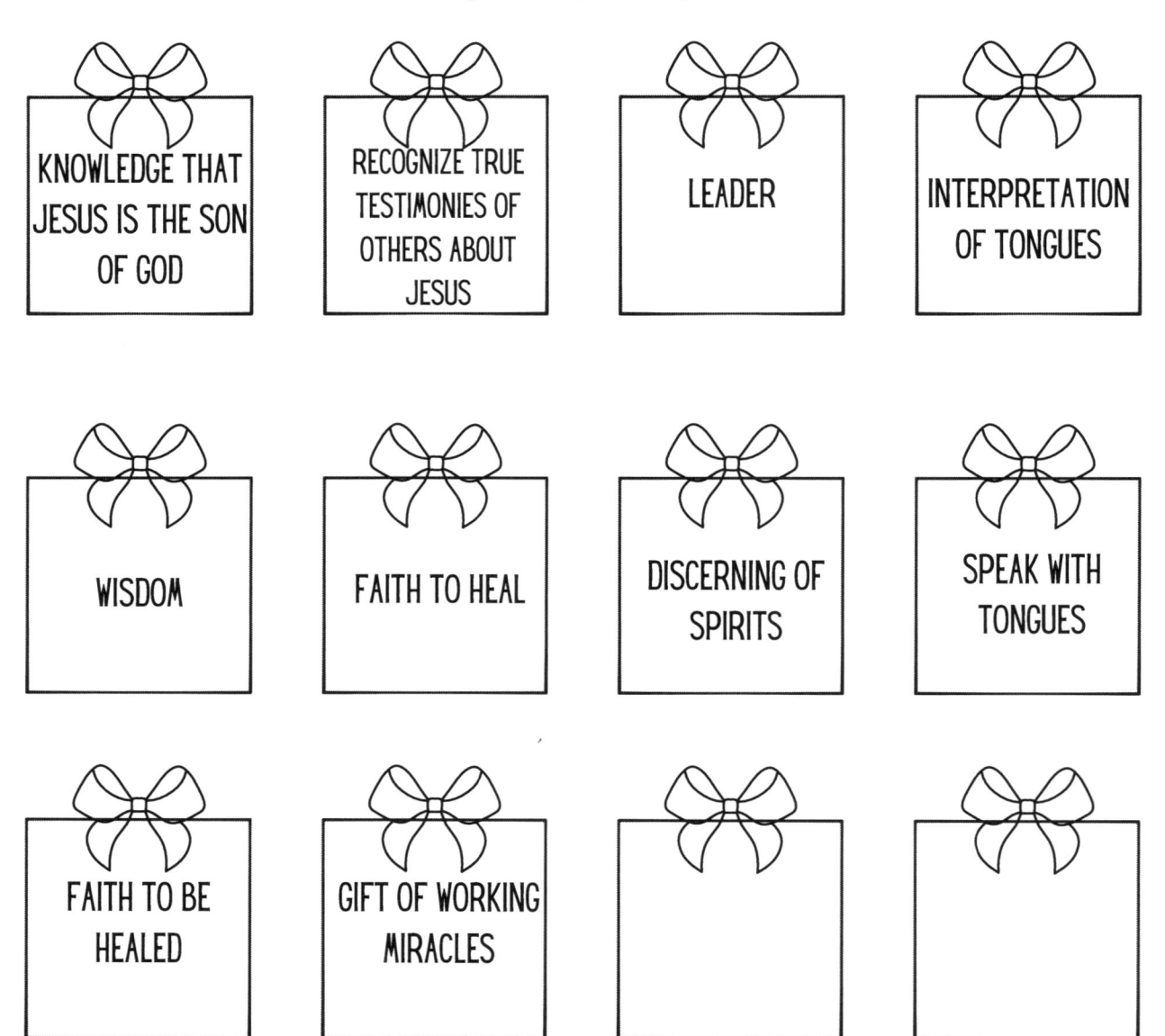

- KNOWLEDGE THAT JESUS IS THE SON OF GOD
- RECOGNIZE TRUE TESTIMONIES OF OTHERS ABOUT JESUS
- LEADER
- INTERPRETATION OF TONGUES
- WISDOM
- FAITH TO HEAL
- DISCERNING OF SPIRITS
- SPEAK WITH TONGUES
- FAITH TO BE HEALED
- GIFT OF WORKING MIRACLES

I HAVE BEEN GIVEN SPIRITUAL GIFTS TO BLESS OTHERS

D&C 46-48

In D&C 47:1,3, we learn about the importance of keeping a history. Why do you think it is important to keep a history of your life? In the box below, write or draw a picture of something that happened this week you would like your grandchildren to know someday. Did you see the hand of the Lord in your life this week?

SOMETHING SPECIAL THAT HAPPENED THIS WEEK

MAY 19-25

CIRCLE THE DAYS YOU READ THIS WEEK: MON TUES WED THUR FRI SAT SUN

In D&C 49:12-14, we read of ways we can follow Jesus Christ. Find some of these ways as you complete the crossword puzzle below.

DOWN

1- THIS IS ANOTHER WORD FOR FAITH IN JESUS

2- THIS MEMBER OF THE GODHEAD HELPS GUIDE US THROUGH PROMPTINGS

ACROSS

3- THIS IS THE FIRST ORDINANCE OF THE GOSPEL WE MUST DO TO RECEIVE SALVATION

4- WE SHOULD DO THIS AFTER WE MAKE A MISTAKE

I CAN FOLLOW JESUS

D&C 49-50

In D&C 50:23-25, we learn about how we can tell if something is of God ("light") or not of God ("darkness"). In the picture below, find the hidden objects that produce light.

THINGS OF GOD BRING US "LIGHT"

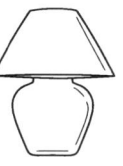

MAY 26-JUNE 1

CIRCLE THE DAYS YOU READ THIS WEEK: MON TUES WED THUR FRI SAT SUN

In D&C 51:9, we learn the Lord wants us to be honest. What are some ways you can choose to be honest? How many words can you make using the letters from words "I can be honest"?

I CAN BE HONEST

_____   _____

_____   _____

_____   _____

_____   _____

_____   _____

_____   _____

_____   _____

_____   *IT FEELS GOOD TO BE HONEST*

_____

D&C 51-57

In D&C 52:14-19, we learn the Lord will give us a "pattern in all things" to help us avoid deception. What are some examples of people trying to deceive us today? These verses help us see that those the Lord calls will always obey the ordinances of the Gospel. Draw or color a pattern on the quilt below.

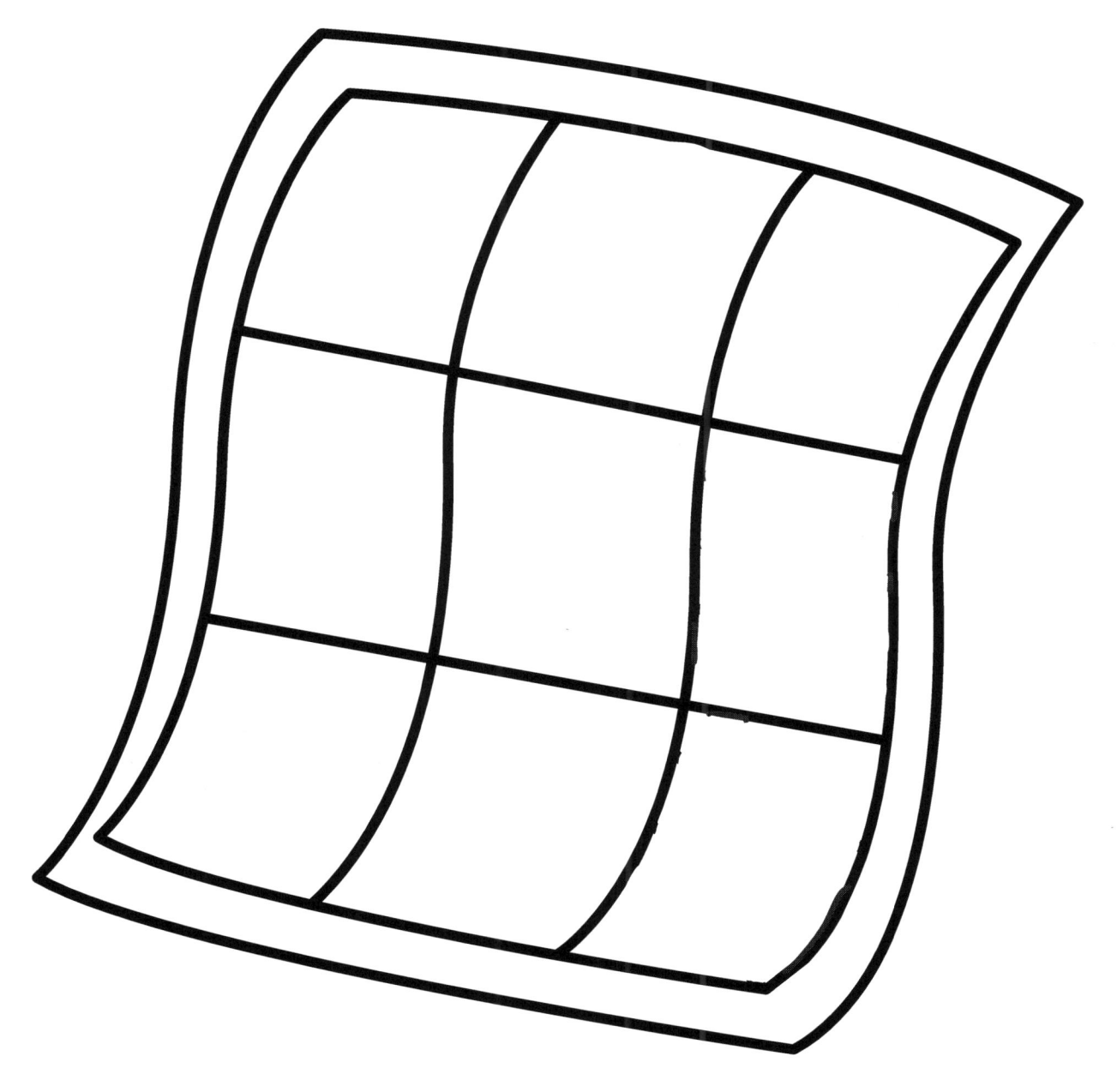

GOD HAS A PATTERN TO HELP ME NOT BE DECEIVED

JUNE 2-8

CIRCLE THE DAYS YOU READ THIS WEEK: MON TUES WED THUR FRI SAT SUN

In D&C 58:26-28, we learn that we have the power to make our own choices. Write the consequences of each of the choices listed below.

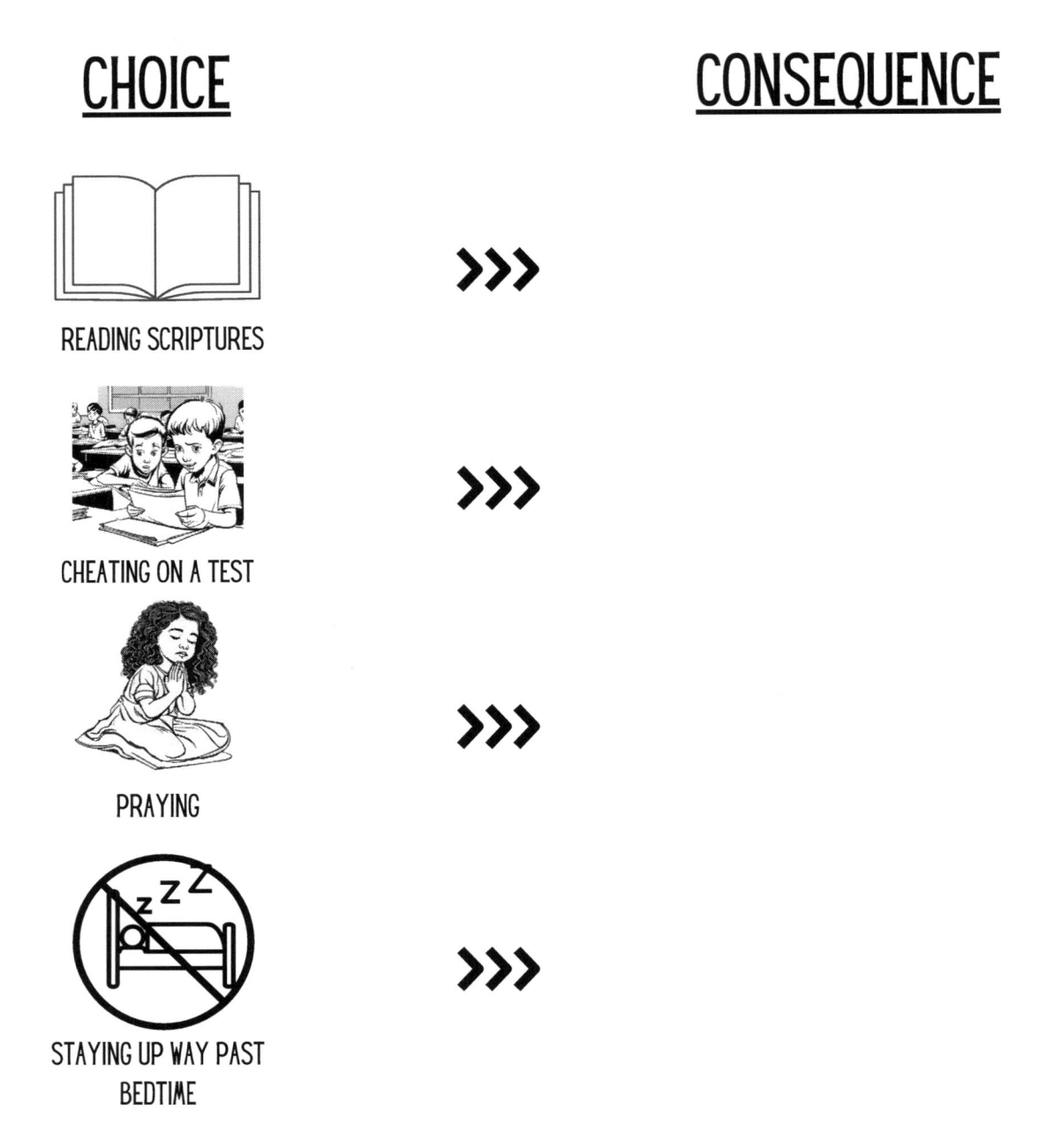

CHOICE   CONSEQUENCE

READING SCRIPTURES »»»

CHEATING ON A TEST »»»

PRAYING »»»

STAYING UP WAY PAST BEDTIME »»»

HEAVENLY FATHER LET'S ME MAKE MY OWN CHOICES

D&C 58-59

In D&C 59:9-12, we learn about keeping the Sabbath Day holy. Complete the word search below that includes words related to keeping the Sabbath holy.

```
Y L P L E S S O N Y O T N X T
U E H Y Z W D Q V A R H S L T
M G C K Q K N G M F U V J J H
S C R I P T U R E S Q J V O D
D Q U C O G S Z M I W M X U F
E P H I J V A S X E I W Y R C
W Q C H Y Y C K O P P X D N W
V L C R K R R L H G J E V A I
F S A I H T A B B A S M E L K
P G S D B V M M R I J O M T J
G F N V J G E O I R J U V J U
J R N X F B N V S R S W X O R
Z Z V I S I T H M I P X Q U L
M T Z K Q G A E C N V V L F H
E C K H E E S Y T O I S K N L
```

SABBATH	CHURCH	SACRAMENT
PRIMARY	SCRIPTURES	LESSON
MUSIC	JOURNAL	VISIT

THE SABBATH DAY IS THE LORD'S DAY

JUNE 9-15

CIRCLE THE DAYS YOU READ THIS WEEK: MON TUES WED THUR FRI SAT SUN

In D&C 60-62, we learn truths about Jesus. Color the picture of Jesus below.

THE SCRIPTURES TEACH OF JESUS

D&C 60-63

In D&C 63:64, we learn about treating sacred things with reverence. Color the boys below that are being reverent.

Walking, not running, through the church halls and using a quiet voice

Pestering your sibling while the sacrament is being passed

Taking the Lord's name in vain

Sitting quietly and listening to your primary teacher during class

Leaving your trash from lunch on the ground at the park

Listening and paying attention to General Conference

Complaining about family scripture study

Eating junk food constantly and not brushing your teeth

I CAN BE REVERENT

JUNE 16-22

CIRCLE THE DAYS YOU READ THIS WEEK: MON TUES WED THUR FRI SAT SUN

In D&C 64:34, we learn that Jesus wants us to follow Him with our hearts and a "willing mind". How can we give our thoughts (minds) and desires (hearts) to the Lord? Count the number of brains and hearts below and then write if they are equal or which one is greater than or less than the other.

# of brains (minds)   < > =   # of hearts

I CAN FOLLOW JESUS WITH MY HEART AND MY MIND

brain - 27; heart 27

D&C 64-66

In D&C 64:7-10, we learn that Jesus wants us to forgive everyone. Forgiving does not mean allowing people to hurt us. Always let a trusted adult know if someone is hurting you. Discuss with your family examples of when you had to forgive. Complete the word search below.

WHO SHOULD I FORGIVE?

START

EVERYONE

JESUS WANTS ME TO FORGIVE EVERYONE

JUNE 23-29

CIRCLE THE DAYS YOU READ THIS WEEK: MON TUES WED THUR FRI SAT SUN

In D&C 67, we read that the revelations Joseph Smith had received were published in a book called The Book of Commandments. We have four books of scripture, which we call the Standard Works, that we can read and study to learn about Jesus. Match each book below with the correct description.

THE BIBLE

THE BOOK OF MORMON

THE PEARL OF GREAT PRICE

THE DOCTRINE AND COVENANTS

RECORD OF THE ANCIENT PEOPLE WHO LIVED IN THE AMERICAS THAT TESTIFIES OF CHRIST.

A BOOK THAT CONTAINS LATTER-DAY REVELATIONS & DECLARATIONS.

A BOOK THAT CONTAINS EXCERPTS FROM JOSEPH SMITH'S TRANSLATION OF GENESIS, MATTHEW 24, TRANSLATION OF SOME EGYPTIAN PAPYRUS (BOOK OF ABRAHAM), AND AN EXCERPT FROM JOSEPH SMITH'S HISTORY.

THIS BOOK CONTAINS THE OLD AND NEW TESTAMENT AND IS A COLLECTION OF WRITINGS BY PROPHETS TESTIFYING OF JESUS.

THE SCRIPTURES TEACH ME ABOUT JESUS

D&C 67-70

In D&C 68:25-31, we learn that we can be baptized once we turn eight years old. Spot and circle the five differences between the two pictures below.

WHAT DIFFERENCES DO YOU SPOT?

WE CAN BE BAPTIZED WHEN WE ARE 8 YEARS OLD

JUNE 30–JULY 6

CIRCLE THE DAYS YOU READ THIS WEEK: MON TUES WED THUR FRI SAT SUN

In D&C 72:2, we learn about a person who is called to help us. Crack the code to find out who this person is.

CRACK THE CODE

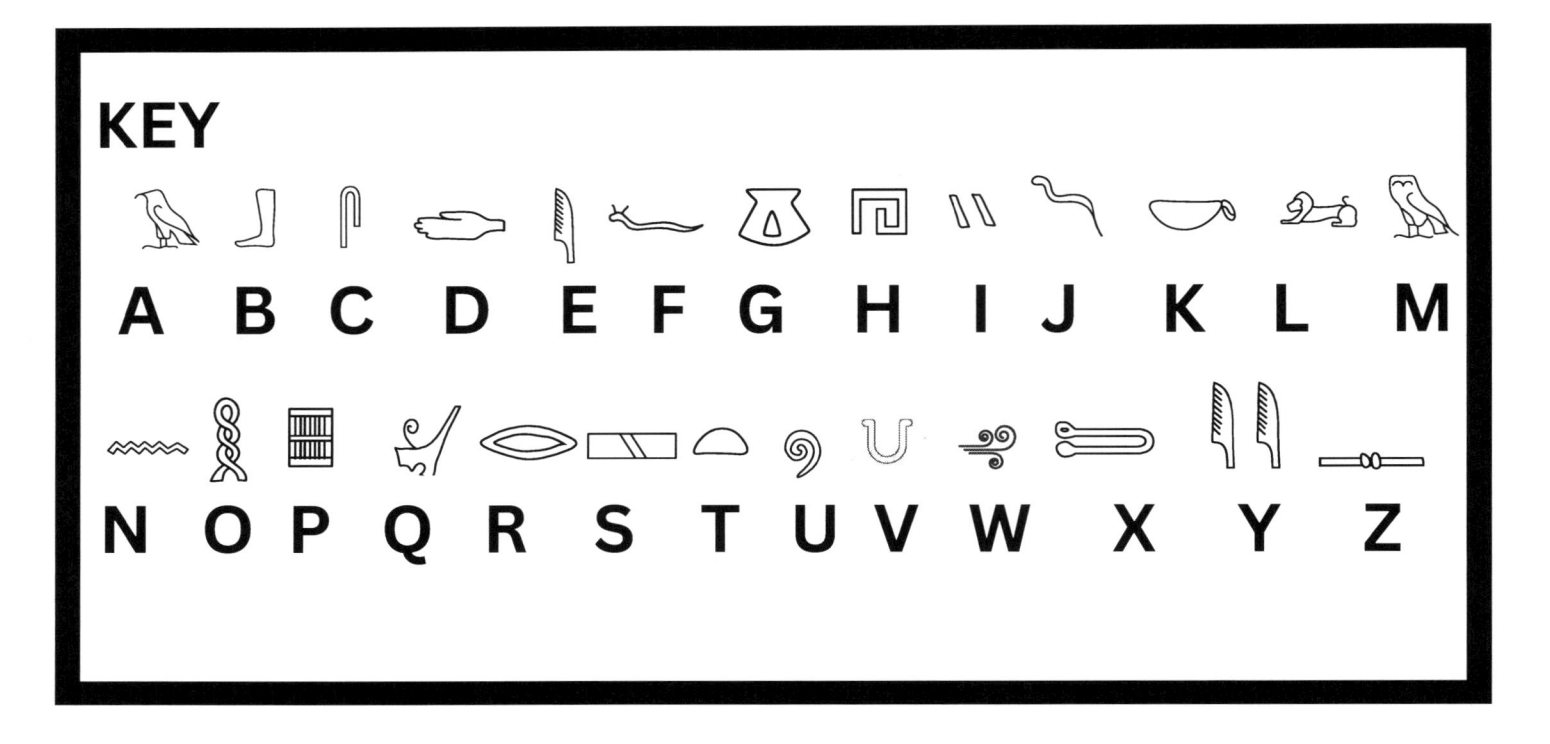

KEY

A B C D E F G H I J K L M
N O P Q R S T U V W X Y Z

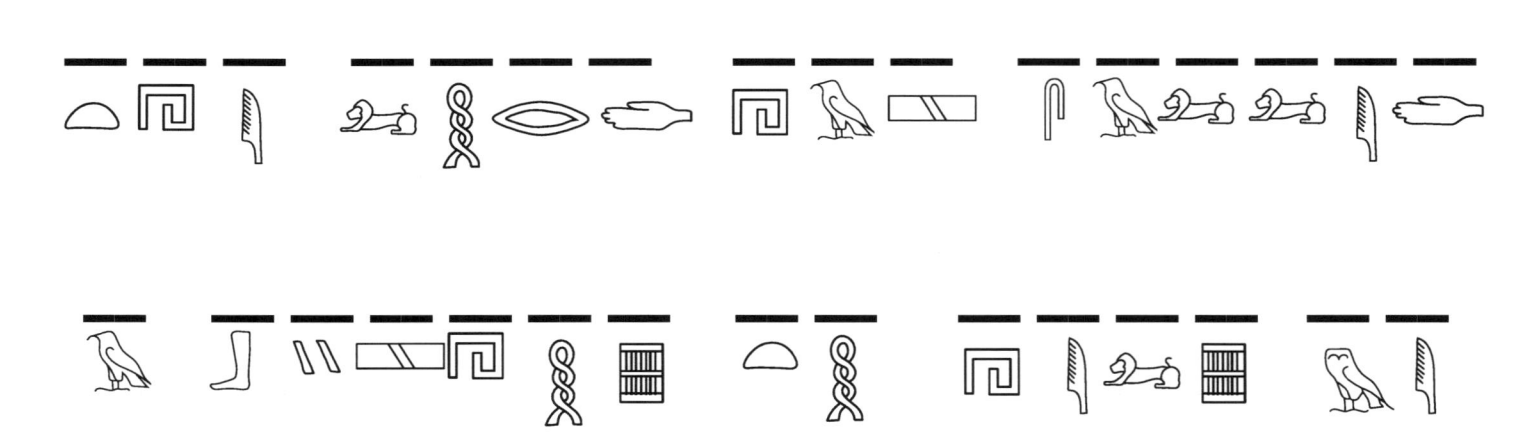

THE BISHOP

A COMMON JUDGE IN ISRAEL

D&C 71-75

In D&C 75:3, we learn that we should give our best efforts to the Lord and not be "idle" (lazy). Give some examples of being idle as well as "labor[ing] with all your might" in the boxes below. Color the pictures.

EXAMPLES OF BEING IDLE:
_____
_____
_____
_____
_____
_____
_____

EXAMPLES OF LABORING WITH ALL YOUR MIGHT:
_____
_____
_____
_____
_____
_____
_____
_____

I CAN GIVE MY BEST EFFORT TO THE LORD

JULY 7-13

CIRCLE THE DAYS YOU READ THIS WEEK: MON TUES WED THUR FRI SAT SUN

In D&C 76, we learn about the three degrees of glory and God's Plan of Salvation. Match each degree of glory with the description of the relationship the people had with Christ below.

CELESTIAL KINGDOM

THOSE WHO REJECTED CHRIST AND HIS GOSPEL; PEOPLE WHO WERE MURDERERS, LIARS, THIEVES, ADULTERERS

TERRESTRIAL KINGDOM

RECEIVED A TESTIMONY OF CHRIST, MADE AND KEPT COVENANTS WITH CHRIST

TELESTIAL KINGDOM

HONORABLE PEOPLE "WHO WERE BLINDED BY THE CRAFTINESS OF MEN" - REJECTED CHRIST ON EARTH BUT ACCEPTED HIM IN SPIRIT WORLD

HEAVENLY FATHER WANTS ME TO RETURN TO LIVE WITH HIM FOREVER

D&C 76; VOICES OF THE RESTORATION: TESTIMONIES OF "THE VISION"

In D&C 76:22-24, we learn we are all sons and daughters of God. Complete the scripture verses below with the correct words. Color the picture.

AND NOW, AFTER THE MANY TESTIMONIES WHICH HAVE BEEN GIVEN OF HIM, THIS IS THE _____, LAST OF ALL, WHICH WE GIVE OF HIM: THAT HE _____! FOR WE SAW _____, EVEN ON THE _____ HAND OF GOD; AND WE HEARD THE _____ BEARING RECORD THAT HE IS THE _____ BEGOTTEN OF THE FATHER—THAT BY HIM, AND THROUGH HIM, AND OF HIM, THE _____ ARE AND WERE CREATED, AND THE INHABITANTS THEREOF ARE BEGOTTEN _____ AND _____ UNTO GOD.
-D&C 76:22-24

LIVES   SONS   ONLY   RIGHT   HIM   VOICE   WORLDS   DAUGHTERS   TESTIMONY

WE ARE ALL CHILDREN OF GOD

JULY 14-20

CIRCLE THE DAYS YOU READ THIS WEEK: MON TUES WED THUR FRI SAT SUN

In D&C 77:2, we read that God created beasts, creeping things, and fowls of the air. Color each group of creatures with it's corresponding color below.

COLOR "BEASTS" (MAMMALS) - BLUE
COLOR "FOWLS OF THE AIR" - YELLOW
COLOR "CREEPING THINGS" - GREEN
(CREATURES THAT GLIDE OR ANIMALS WITHOUT BACKBONE (INSECTS, WORMS, CRABS, ETC))

GOD CREATED EVERY CREATURE ON THE EARTH

D&C 77-80

In D&C 78:6, we learn we must share with those in need. In the box below, draw a picture of things you have that you could share with others. Make a plan with your family to give items to those in need.

I CAN SHARE WITH THOSE IN NEED

JULY 21-27

CIRCLE THE DAYS YOU READ THIS WEEK: MON TUES WED THUR FRI SAT SUN

In D&C 81:3, we learn that we can pray to God both, out loud and in our hearts. Color the picture of the girl praying below and write three things you can pray for inside the hearts.

I CAN PRAY VOCALLY AND IN MY HEART

D&C 81-83

In D&C 81:5, we read that we should help those in need. Jesus was the perfect example of helping the weak. With your family or primary class, think of examples from the scriptures of Jesus helping others. In the top row, write what the pictures could be showing. In the bottom squares, draw or write your own examples of ways Jesus helped others.

JESUS HELPED THOSE IN NEED & I CAN, TOO

JULY 28-AUGUST 3

CIRCLE THE DAYS YOU READ THIS WEEK: MON TUES WED THUR FRI SAT SUN

In D&C 84:19-22, we learn about the importance of priesthood ordinances. Fill in the missing words from D&C 84:20-22 below.

THEREFORE, IN THE _____ THEREOF, THE _____ OF GODLINESS IS MANIFEST. AND WITHOUT THE ORDINANCES THEREOF, AND THE _____ OF THE _____, THE POWER OF _____ IS NOT MANIFEST UNTO MEN IN THE _____; FOR WITHOUT THIS NO _____ CAN SEE THE FACE OF _____, EVEN THE FATHER AND _____
-D&C 84:20-22

GODLINESS   ORDINANCE   POWER   AUTORITY   LIVE   PRIESTHOOD   FLESH   MAN   GOD   POWER

Unscramble the words below that are priesthood ordinances. Other ordinances not listed below include ordaining to priesthood offices, consecrating oil, administering to the sick, anointing with oil, sealing the anointing, Father's blessings, blessings of comfort and guidance, and dedicating graves.

SBPTIMA _____

ACSAMETRN _____

ONIRMTCIONFA _____

I CAN RECEIVE HEAVENLY FATHER'S POWER THROUGH PRIESTHOOD ORDINANCES

D&C 84

In D&C 84:77, Jesus calls us his friends. What makes a good friend? How can you be a good friend to Jesus? Help the person below make his way through the maze to Jesus.

I CAN BE A FRIEND TO JESUS BY FOLLOWING HIM

AUGUST 4-10

CIRCLE THE DAYS YOU READ THIS WEEK: MON TUES WED THUR FRI SAT SUN

In D&C 86, we learn more about the parable of the wheat and the tares described in Matthew 13. We can help gather the "wheat" (God's people). Match the pictures to the correct definition below as you read D&C 86.

WHEAT

TARES

FIELD

SOWER OF SEEDS

THE ENEMY

THE HARVEST

THOSE WHO FOLLOW SATAN

CHRIST AND HIS APOSTLES

THE RIGHTEOUS

THE WORLD

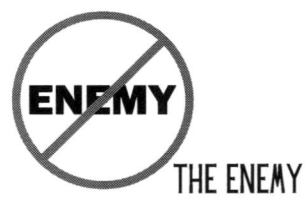

END OF THE WORLD

THE DEVIL & HIS POWER

I CAN GATHER GOD'S PEOPLE

D&C 85-87

In D&C 87:8, the Lord tells us to stand in holy places. How can we make our homes a holy place? Write or draw things that will make your home holy in the house below.

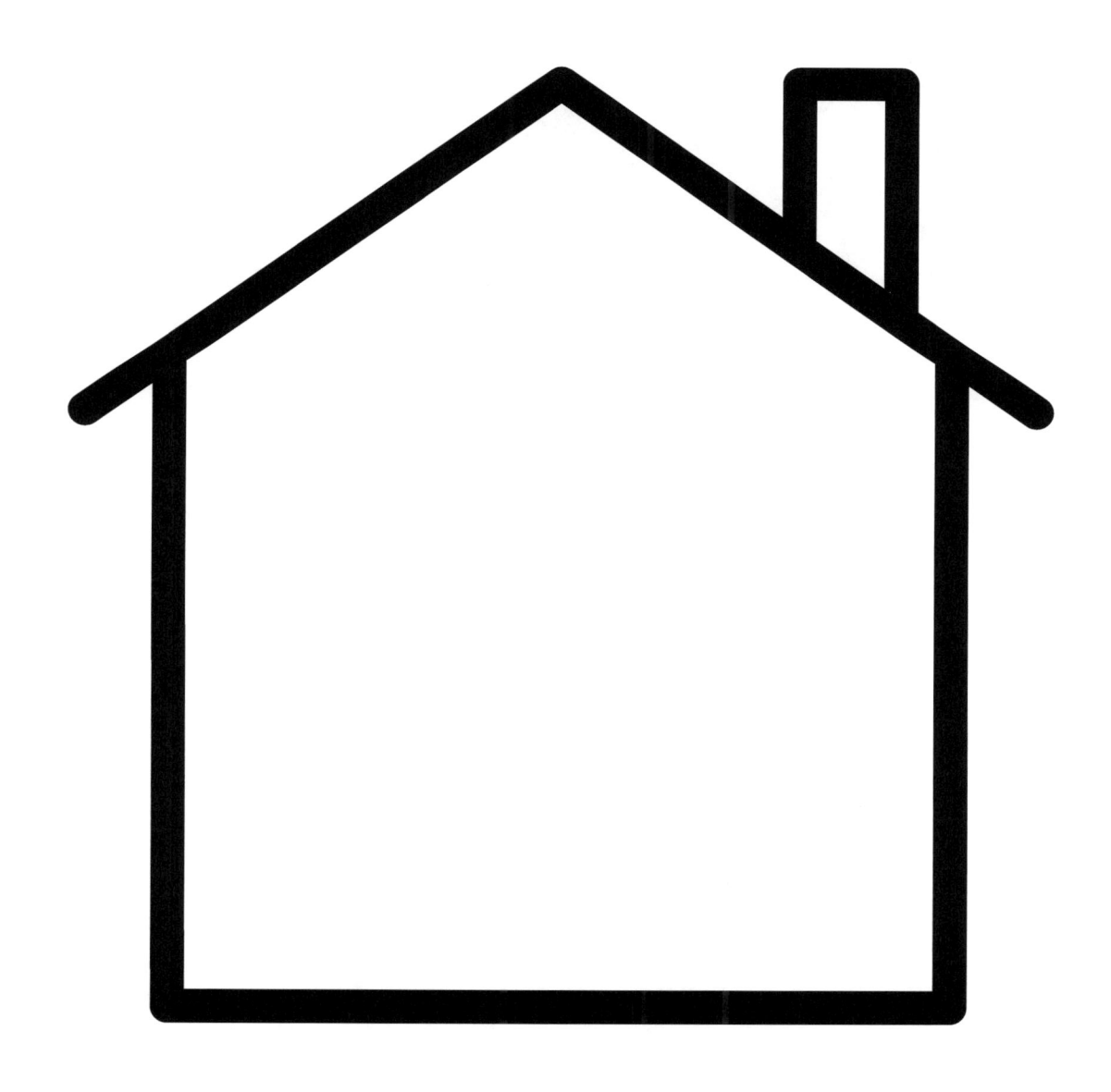

I CAN MAKE MY HOME A HOLY PLACE

AUGUST 11-17

CIRCLE THE DAYS YOU READ THIS WEEK: MON TUES WED THUR FRI SAT SUN

In D&C 88:77-80, 118, we learn that it is important to the Lord that we learn. Write or draw answers to the questions below.

WHAT THE LORD WANTS ME TO LEARN
D&C 88:77-79

WHY HE WANTS ME TO LEARN
D&C 88:80

HOW WE SHOULD LEARN
D&C 88:118

HEAVENLY FATHER WANTS ME TO LEARN

D&C 88

In D&C 88:119, Joseph was told to establish a House of God. We can make our homes like the temple. Find words from this scripture in the word search below.

```
O R D E R T S N V C K A P I B
O S M L O S H M U Z C C O X Z
S Y M H C Q O R G A N I Z E V
Z C L A W X U G Y S Y I C M D
A J E Z B V S W R O R K M T S
M L S K K D E T O B B K B V N
Z D T N N E F A S T I N G J C
Y Y A Y S C J D G E V E A Z Z
K F B C C I J G F L B F M L Q
O E L E A R N I N G O R B J I
D I I Y R A P R A Y E R T S Q
V V S N T Q M U D N S Z Y M G
G M H F W P R Q C L A K C I G
D S Y S T F A I T H P M R E O
F W H F F R W I T K A N Q V D
```

ORGANIZE	ESTABLISH	HOUSE
PRAYER	FASTING	FAITH
LEARNING	GLORY	ORDER
GOD		

OUR HOMES CAN BE LIKE THE TEMPLE

AUGUST 18-24

CIRCLE THE DAYS YOU READ THIS WEEK: MON TUES WED THUR FRI SAT SUN

In D&C 89, the Lord gives us a Word of Wisdom to keep our bodies and spirits healthy. A good way to avoid temptation is to make a plan now on how you would respond when you are offered something that is against the Word of Wisdom. Answer the questions below.

HOW WOULD YOU RESPOND TO A FRIEND THAT OFFERS TO LET YOU TRY "JUST A SIP" OF BEER OR ALCOHOL?

HOW WOULD YOU RESPOND TO A FRIEND THAT PRESSURES YOU TO TRY VAPING?

A FRIEND OFFERS YOU AN ICED COFFEE. WHAT DO YOU SAY?

THE WORD OF WISDOM KEEPS MY BODY & SPIRIT HEALTHY

To read more info on parts of the Word of Wisdom youth may be confused about, visit https://www.churchofjesuschrist.org/study/new-era/2019/08/vaping-coffee-tea-and-marijuana

D&C 89-92

In D&C 90:5, we learn that the Lord gives us prophets to guide and protect us. Can you name the first presidency and the 12 apostles of the Church of Jesus Christ of Latter-day Saints? Ask your family or primary class for help, if needed.

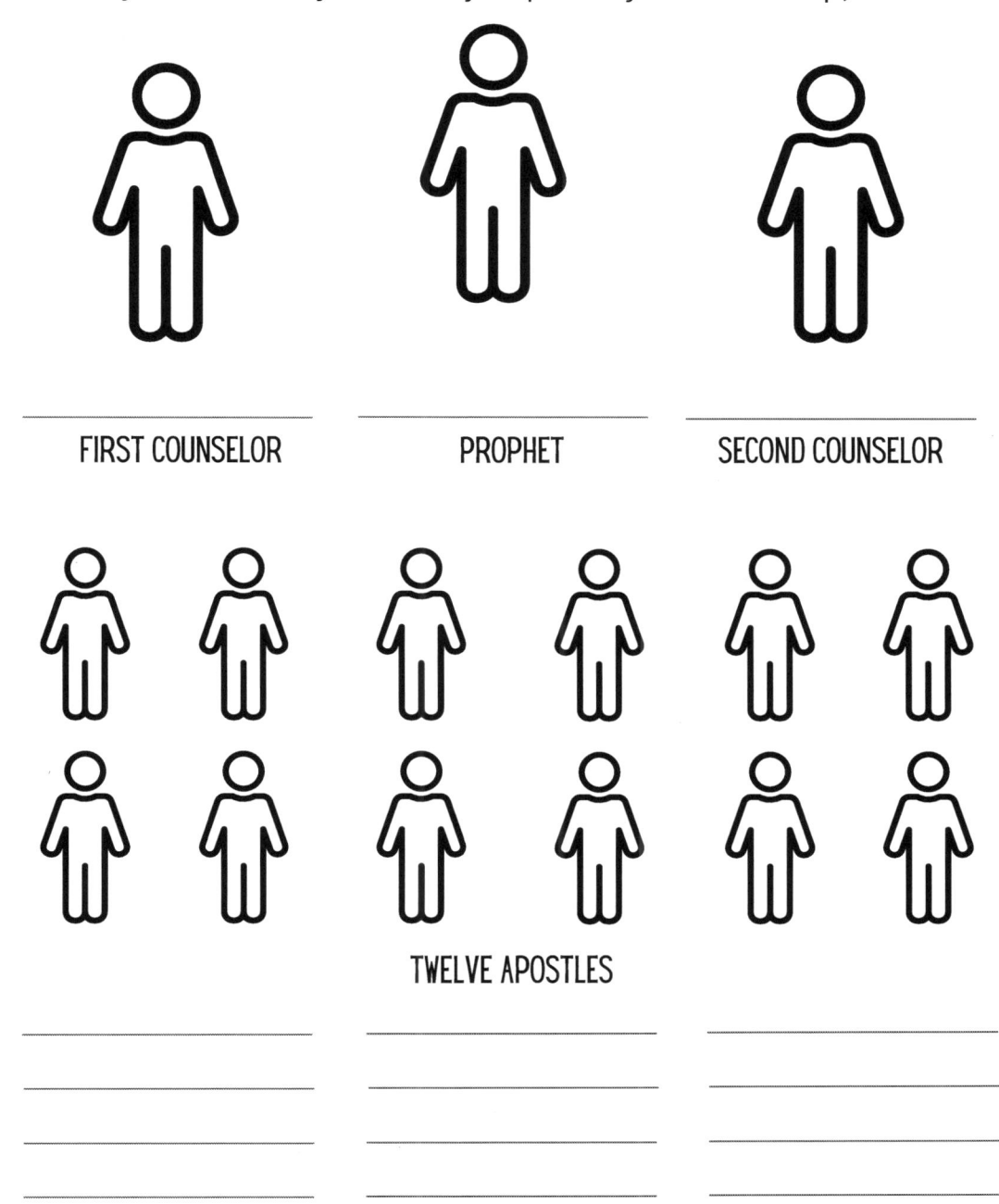

FIRST COUNSELOR   PROPHET   SECOND COUNSELOR

TWELVE APOSTLES

GOD GIVES ME PROPHETS TO GUIDE & PROTECT ME

AUGUST 25-31

CIRCLE THE DAYS YOU READ THIS WEEK: MON TUES WED THUR FRI SAT SUN

In D&C 93:2-21, we learn many important truths about the Savior. One of those truths is listed below, but you must crack the code to figure out what it is.

CRACK THE CODE

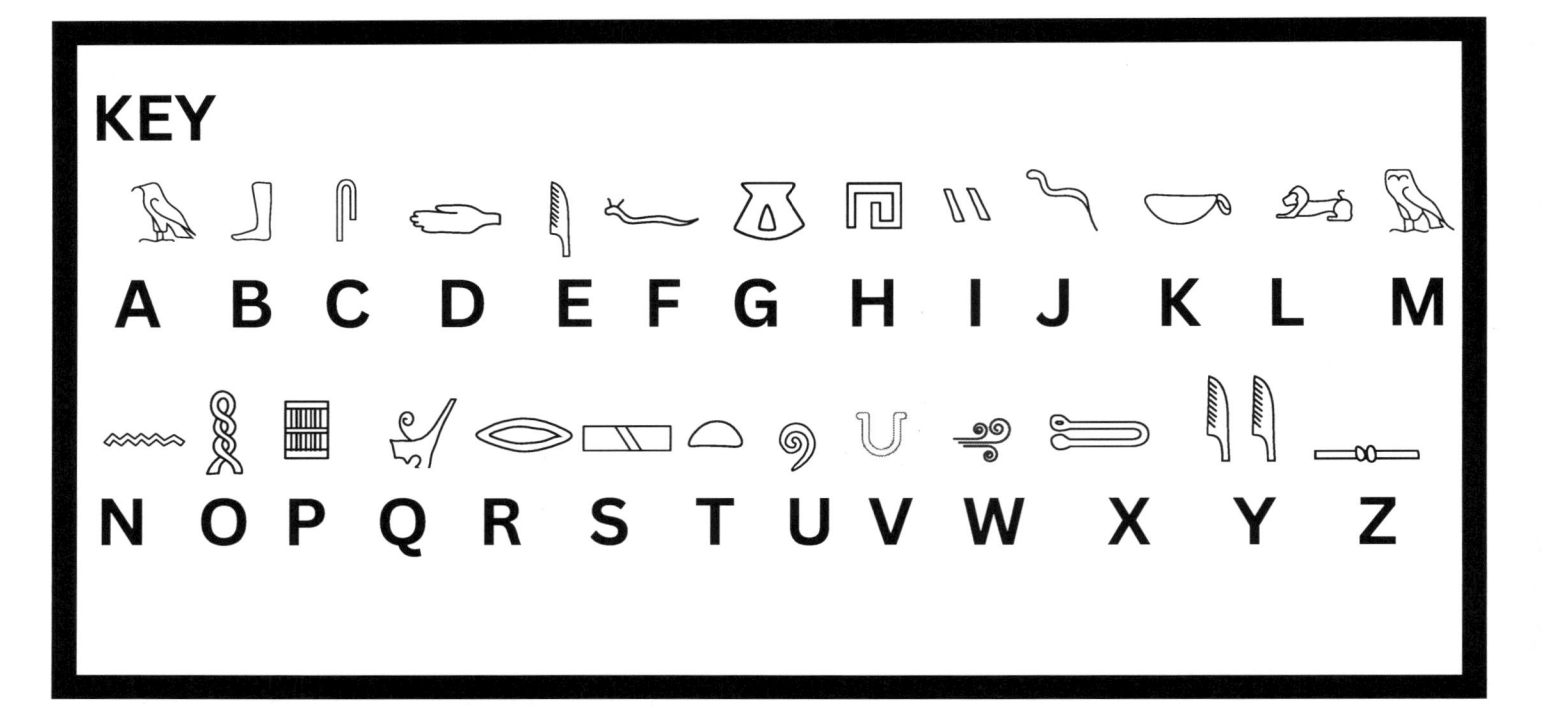

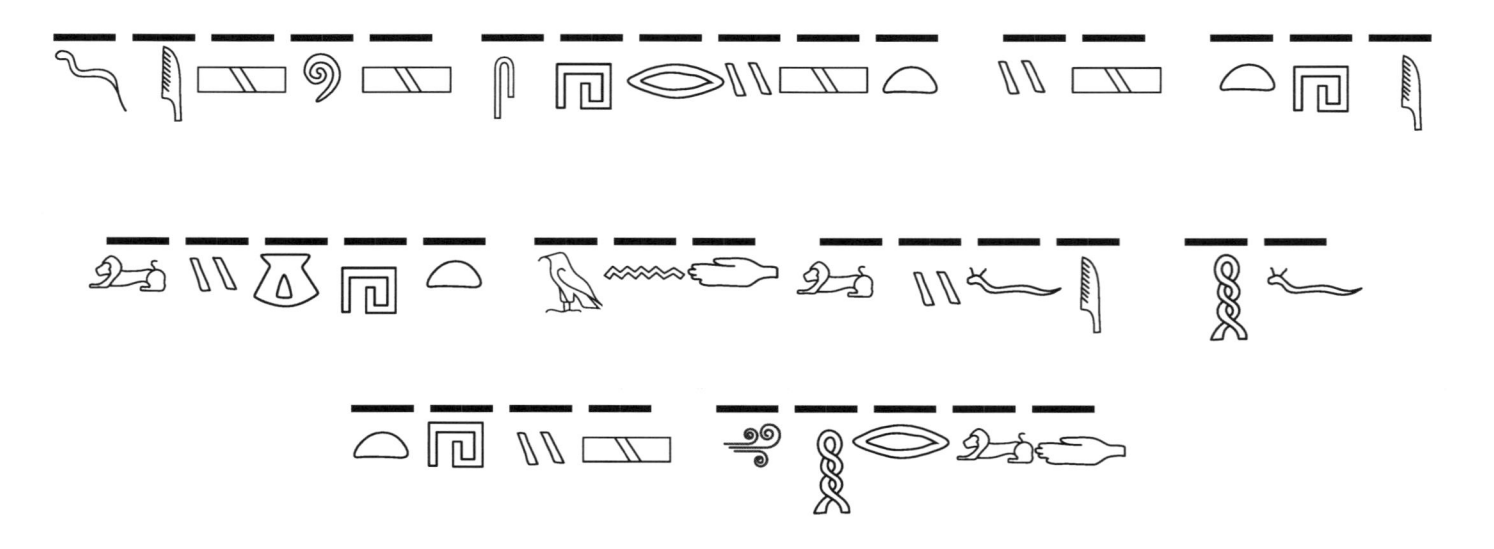

D&C 93

In D&C 93: 23, 29, and 38, we learn that we lived with God before we came to Earth. Count how many clouds you count below.

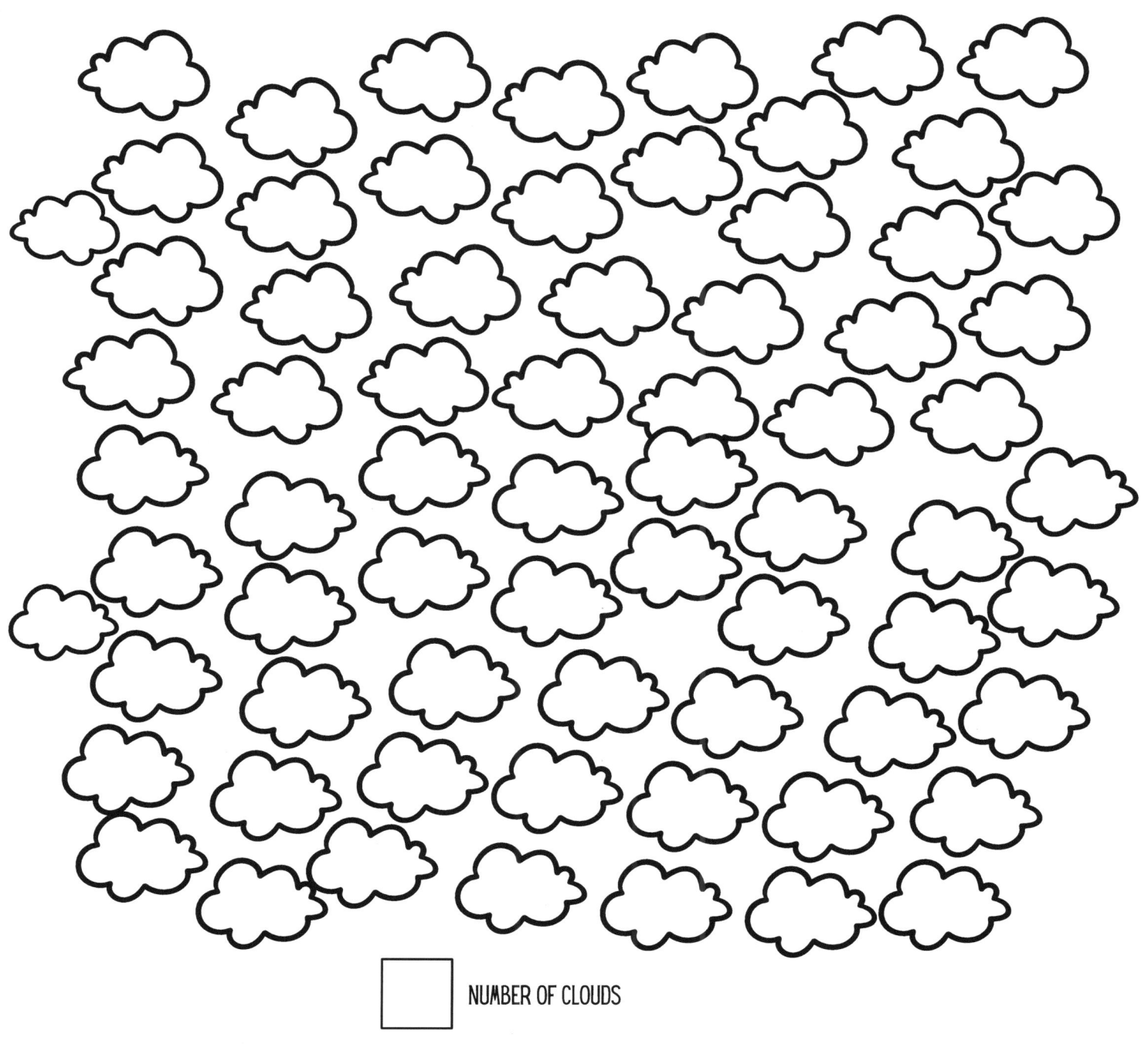

☐ NUMBER OF CLOUDS

I LIVED WITH GOD BEFORE I CAME TO EARTH

ANSWER: 70

SEPTEMBER 1-7

CIRCLE THE DAYS YOU READ THIS WEEK: MON TUES WED THUR FRI SAT SUN

In D&C 97:1–2, 8–9, 21, we learn that Zion is "the pure in heart". What does it mean for your heart to be pure? See how many words you can make out of the phrase "Zion is the pure in heart" below.

ZION IN THE PURE IN HEART

_____   _____

_____   _____

_____   _____

_____   _____

_____   _____

_____   _____

_____   _____

_____   PURE

D&C 94-97

In D&C 95:8, we read why the Lord wants us to build temples. The Kirtland Temple was the first temple in this dispensation. Color the temple below.

THE TEMPLE IS THE HOUSE OF THE LORD

HOUSE OF THE LORD

SEPTEMBER 8-14

CIRCLE THE DAYS YOU READ THIS WEEK: MON TUES WED THUR FRI SAT SUN

In D&C 98:1-3, we learn about trials the Saints in Missouri were experiencing. In 1833, the Saints were driven out through violence. What trials do you have in your life? Have any of your trials every turned to a blessing? Find the hidden pictures below.

JESUS CAN TURN MY TRIALS INTO BLESSINGS

D&C 98-101

In D&C 101:16, we learn that we can find peace when we are still and thinking about Jesus. Help the boy pick the correct path to find peace.

JESUS CAN BRING ME PEACE

SEPTEMBER 15-21

CIRCLE THE DAYS YOU READ THIS WEEK: MON TUES WED THUR FRI SAT SUN

In D&C 105, we learn about Zion's Camp. A group of men from Ohio marched to Missouri to help the Saints there. The Lord told the Saints he wanted them to make peace with those being unkind to them in D&C 105:38-40. Spot and circle the differences between the two pictures below.

SPOT THE 7 DIFFERENCES

I CAN BE A PEACEMAKER

D&C 102-105; VOICES OF THE RESTORATION: ZION'S CAMP

In D&C 103:9, we are told we can be a light to others when we follow Jesus. Color all of the words below that are synonyms of the word "light."

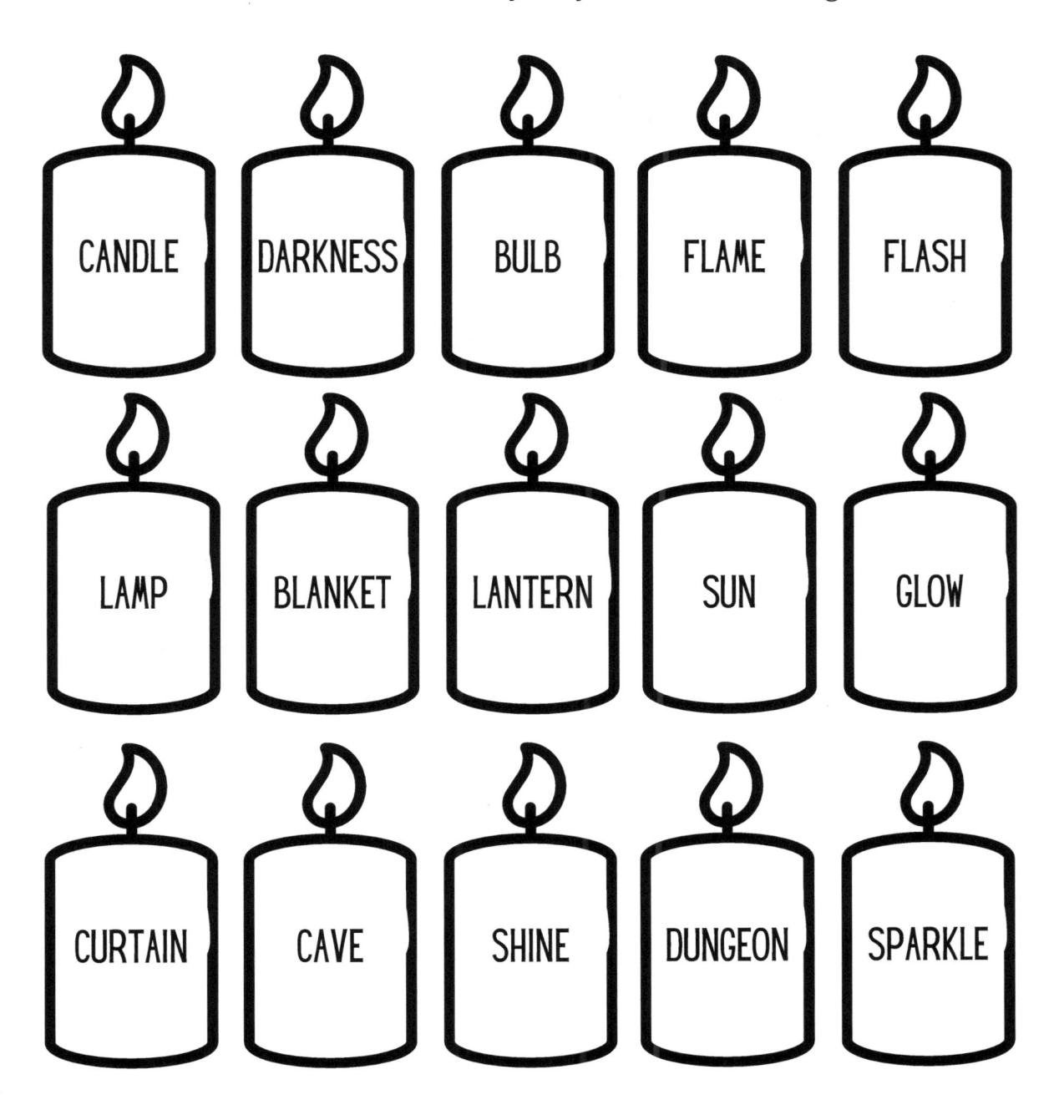

| CANDLE | DARKNESS | BULB | FLAME | FLASH |

| LAMP | BLANKET | LANTERN | SUN | GLOW |

| CURTAIN | CAVE | SHINE | DUNGEON | SPARKLE |

I CAN BE A LIGHT UNTO THE WORLD

SEPTEMBER 22-28

CIRCLE THE DAYS YOU READ THIS WEEK: MON TUES WED THUR FRI SAT SUN

In D&C 107:18-20, we read about the priesthood holds "all the spiritual blessings of the church". Draw or write all of the blessings you can think of that come from the priesthood. Examples of blessings include baptism, eternal families, healing the sick, etc.

JESUS BLESSES ME THROUGH HIS PRIESTHOOD POWER

D&C 106-108

In D&C 108:3, we read that we should be careful in observing our covenants. In the examples below, draw a line to either "careful" or "casual" to decide how the person is behaving in that situation.

LUKE READS THE COME, FOLLOW ME LESSON EACH WEEK & IS PREPARED TO PARTICIPATE IN CLASS & GIVE INSIGHTFUL COMMENTS.

SOFIE WATCHES A TV SHOW HER FRIENDS AT SCHOOL ALWAYS ARE TALKING ABOUT, EVEN THOUGH IT USES INAPPROPRIATE LANGUAGE AND HAS QUESTIONABLE CONTENT.

CAREFUL or **CASUAL**

GREY PLAYS GAMES ON HIS TABLET WHILE THE SACRAMENT IS BEING PASSED.

OLIVIA GETS INTO BED & THEN REMEMBERS SHE FORGOT TO SAY HER PRAYERS. SHE DECIDES SHE WILL JUST DO IT TOMORROW AS SHE IS TOO COMFORTABLE TO KNEEL.

I CAN BE CAREFUL IN LIVING MY COVENANTS

SEPTEMBER 29-OCTOBER 5

CIRCLE THE DAYS YOU READ THIS WEEK: MON TUES WED THUR FRI SAT SUN

In D&C 110, the Lord appeared and accepted the Kirtland Temple as His house. In the hearts below, write things you love about the temple.

THE TEMPLE IS THE HOUSE OF THE LORD

D&C 109-110; VOICES OF THE RESTORATION: SPIRITUAL MANIFESTATIONS & THE KIRTLAND TEMPLE

In D&C 110, we learn of heavenly beings who visited Joseph Smith and Oliver Cowdery in the Kirtland temple and restored priesthood keys. Match the heavenly beings with the priesthood keys they restored.

ELIAS

ELIJAH

MOSES

GATHERING OF ISRAEL

GOSPEL OF ABRAHAM/CELESTIAL MARRIAGE

SEALING POWER

THE SAVIOR BLESSES US THROUGH PRIESTHOOD KEYS

OCTOBER 6-12

CIRCLE THE DAYS YOU READ THIS WEEK: MON TUES WED THUR FRI SAT SUN

In D&C 111:2, 10-11, we read that the things of God can be a treasure to us. On the coins below, color the coins that are "Godly" treasures.

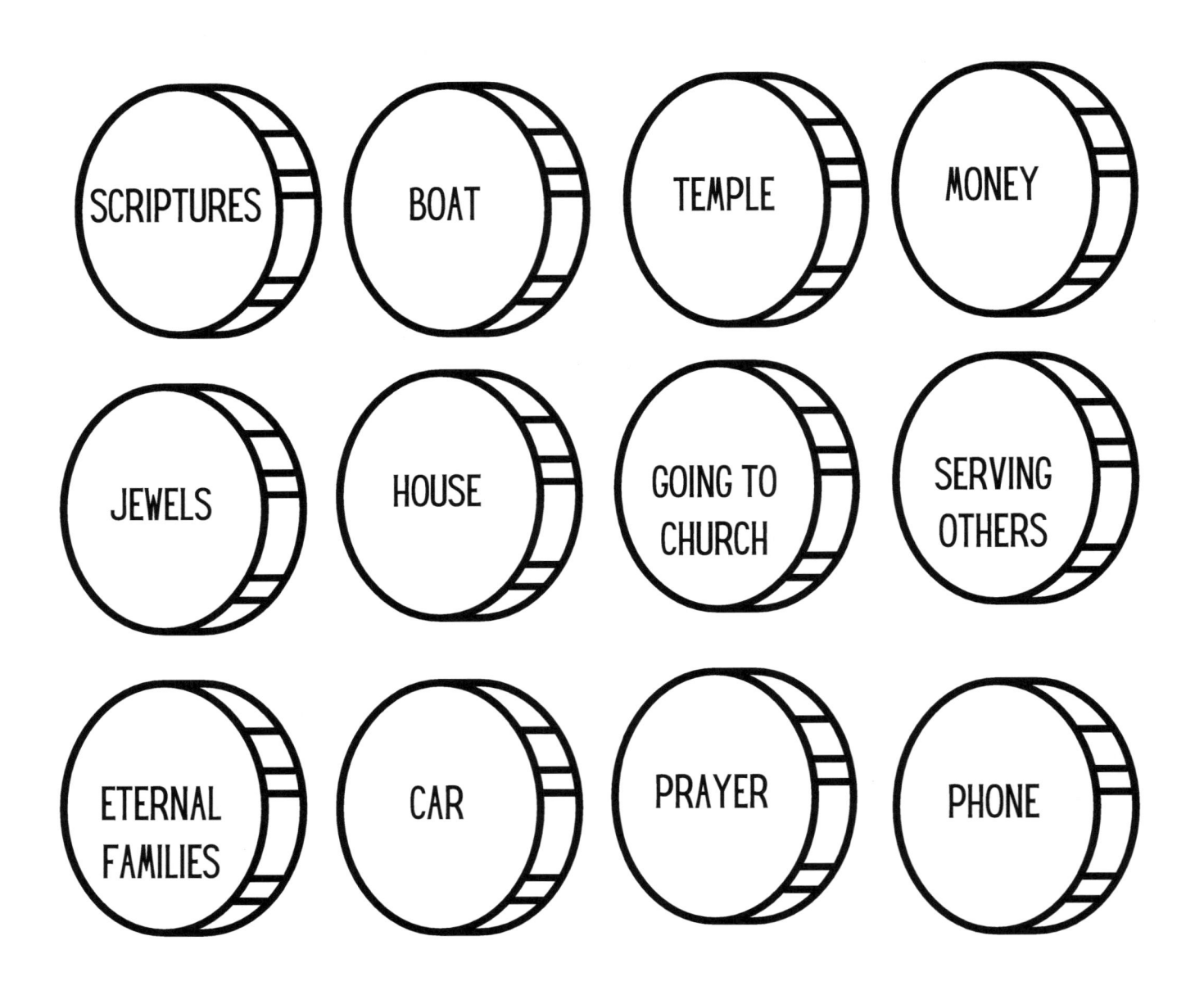

SCRIPTURES	BOAT	TEMPLE	MONEY
JEWELS	HOUSE	GOING TO CHURCH	SERVING OTHERS
ETERNAL FAMILIES	CAR	PRAYER	PHONE

THE THINGS OF GOD ARE A TREASURE TO ME

D&C 111-114

In D&C 112:10, we learn that if we are humble the Lord will lead us and give us answers to our prayers. In D&C 112:11, we learn that we should love everyone. Complete the word search below with words from these verses.

```
K L P Y L O V E V N B A T C A
B E L J T B K L L P T S K M R
T A L K J N M H X X R G S G W
Q D K V Y M E X M E F V Q I D
G H H B I F P P W S V F U Z T
W M Z R L V T S R K M V P F X
V T Z N E E N T O A C T S Q Z
M V Q W L A S T M A Y A C H D
V M R B F G J S I C L E I O M
R A M H J H O P I K R Q R Y V
Y U Y B W W G O F N I P Q S T
H P J Z O Z Y J A T G G G L G
F J C L X V E A W S G S D U I
U H X H A N D T R U S T J E V
E V E R Y O N E F U V C W E E
```

HUMBLE	LEAD	HAND
GIVE	ANSWERS	PRAYER
BLESSINGS	LOVE	EVERYONE

THE LORD WILL LEAD ME BY THE HAND & ANSWER MY PRAYERS

OCTOBER 13-19

CIRCLE THE DAYS YOU READ THIS WEEK: MON TUES WED THUR FRI SAT SUN

In D&C 115:4-5, the Lord names His Church "The Church of Jesus Christ of Latter-day Saints." What is the significance of the name of the Church? Color the picture below.

I belong to the

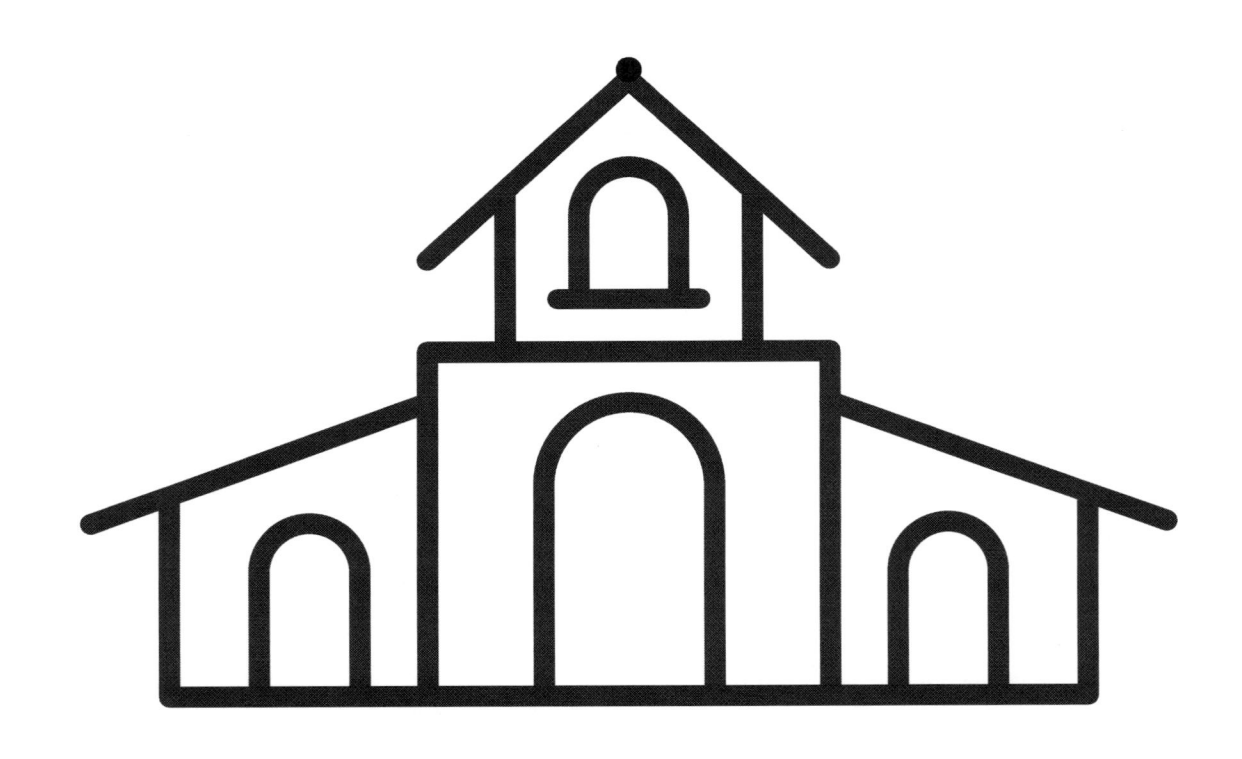

# of Jesus Christ

D&C 115-120

In D&C 119, the Lord gives the Law of Tithing in this section. We are to give one-tenth of our earnings to the Lord. In the circles below, write some ways your tithing is used. Ask your family or primary class for ideas, if needed.

HEAVENLY FATHER USES TITHING TO BLESS HIS CHILDREN

OCTOBER 20-26

CIRCLE THE DAYS YOU READ THIS WEEK: MON TUES WED THUR FRI SAT SUN

Read D&C 121:1-9; 122:7-9. Imagine what it must have been like for Joseph Smith & the five others in Liberty Jail. How can we find peace in life, even during hard trials? In the box below, draw a picture of Joseph, Sydney, Hyrum, Lyman, Caleb, and Alexander in jail.

JESUS HELPED JOSEPH FEEL PEACE IN LIBERTY JAIL

D&C 121-123; VOICES OF THE RESTORATION: LIBERTY JAIL

In D&C 123:15-17, we learn that small things can make a big difference. Like a small helm of a ship steers the big ship, our small efforts can make a big difference. Think of small ways you can serve your family and friends this week and write them in circles below.

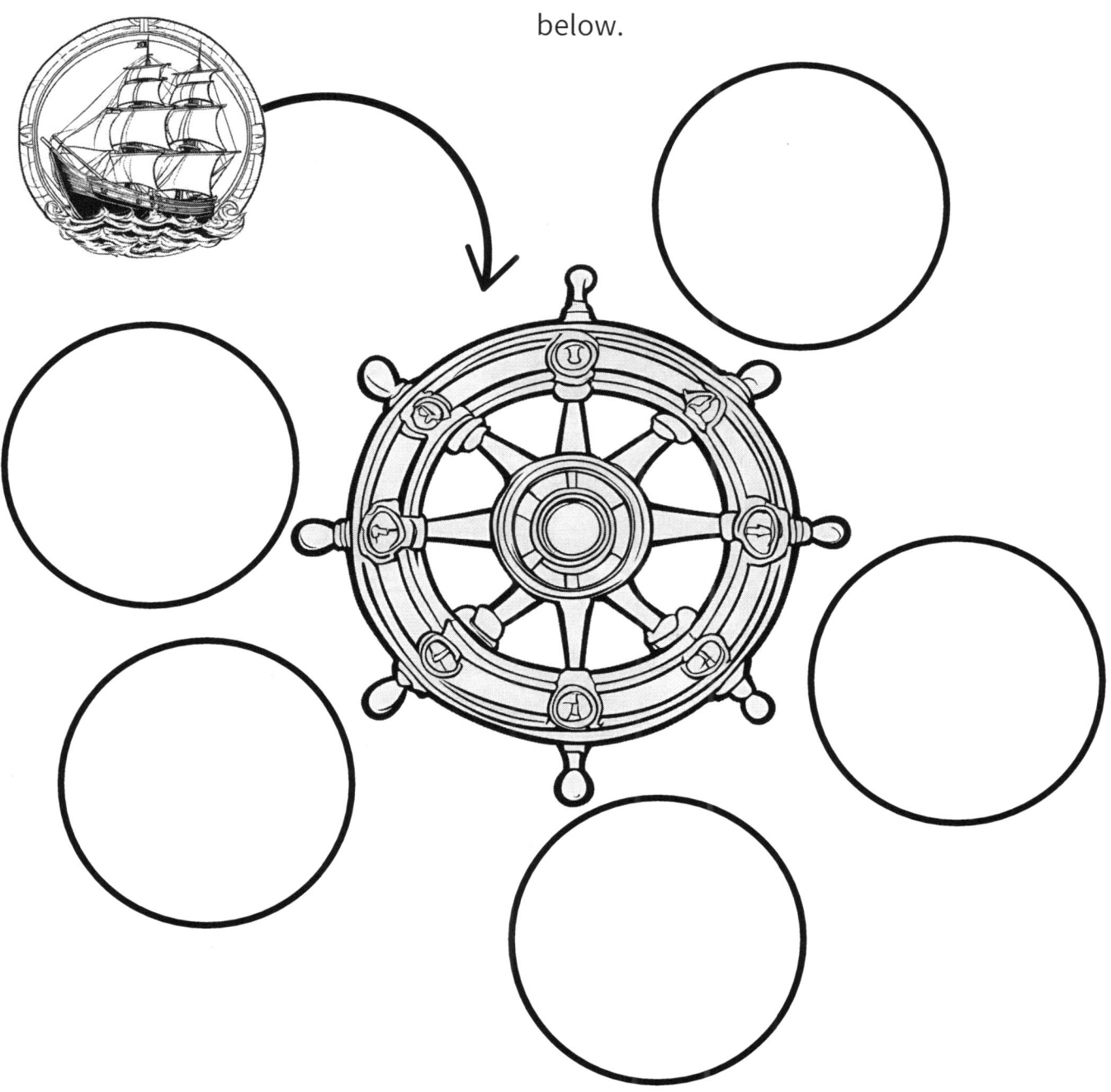

SMALL EFFORTS CAN MAKE A BIG DIFFERENCE

OCTOBER 27-NOVEMBER 2

CIRCLE THE DAYS YOU READ THIS WEEK: MON TUES WED THUR FRI SAT SUN

After facing much persecution in both Kirtland and Missouri, the Saints in Ohio and Missouri left in 1838 and gathered in Illinois. There they built the city of Nauvoo on swampy land next to the Mississippi River. In D&C 124:28-29, 39, the Lord commands the Saints to build a temple in Nauvoo. Draw your own sunstone on the blank column below, using the example above for guidance.

SAINTS GATHER IN NAUVOO

FINISH DRAWING THE SUNSTONE FOR THE NAUVOO TEMPLE

WHAT DO YOU THINK THE SUNSTONES ON THE NAUVOO TEMPLE REPRESENT?

_____
_____
_____

HOW MANY SUNSTONES WERE ON THE OLD & NEW NAUVOO TEMPLE?

_____

JESUS CHRIST COMMANDS HIS PEOPLE TO BUILD TEMPLES

Answer: Sun represents the Restoration & the Gospel bringing light to the Earth; 30 sunstones on both the old and new Nauvoo temples

D&C 124; VOICES OF THE RESTORATION: THE RELIEF SOCIETY

In D&C 124:91-92, we learn about patriarchal blessings. A patriarchal blessing teaches you about yourself, as well as what the Lord would like you to do in your life. Complete the maze below.

ETERNAL LIFE

START

THE LORD CAN GUIDE ME THROUGH MY PATRIARCHAL BLESSING

NOVEMBER 3-9

CIRCLE THE DAYS YOU READ THIS WEEK: MON TUES WED THUR FRI SAT SUN

In D&C 126:3, we learn that we should care for our families and serve them. Can you think of ways you can help care for your family? Color hearts below that describe ways to care for and serve your family.

COLOR THE HEARTS THAT LIST WAYS TO SERVE YOUR FAMILY

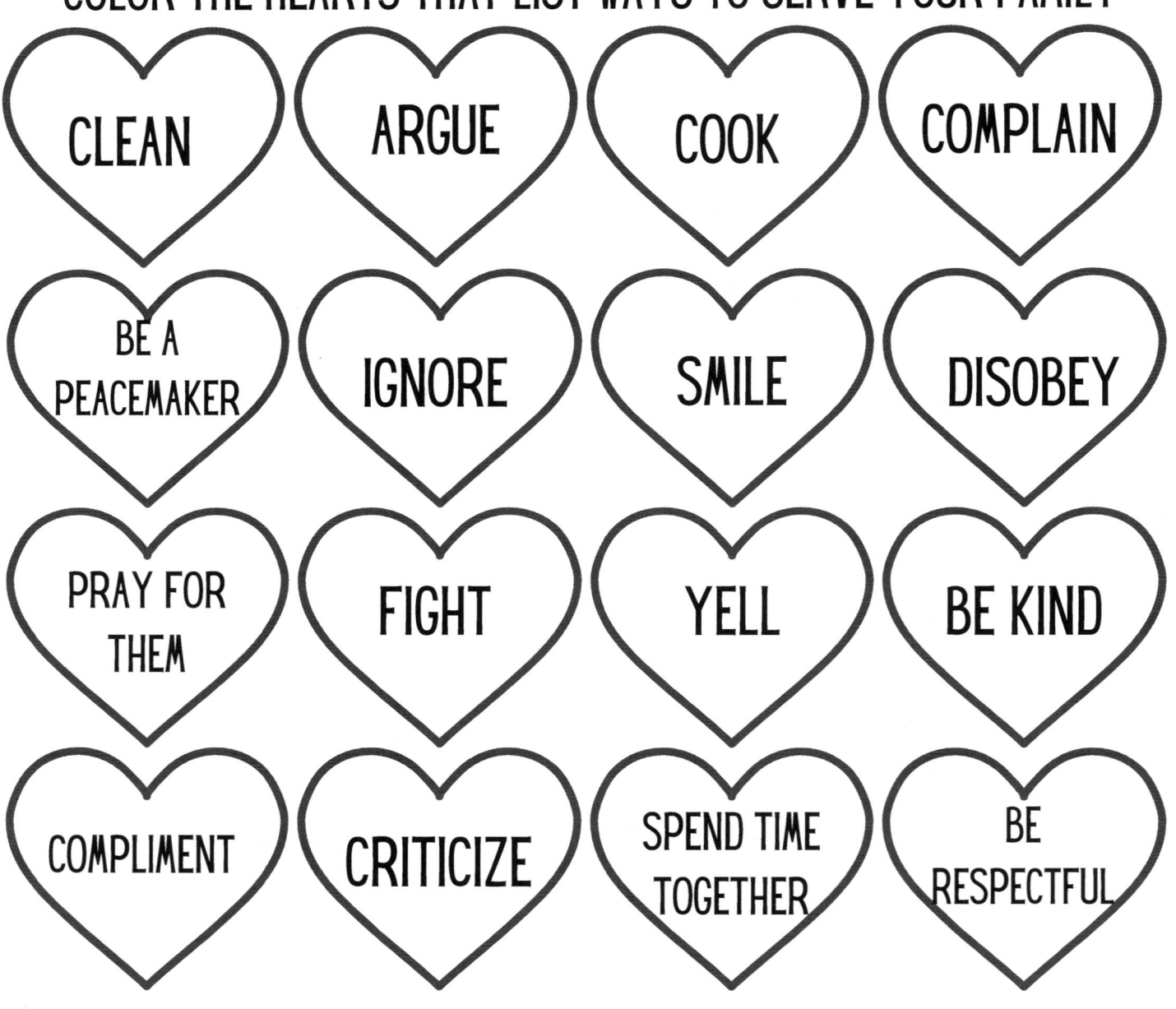

- CLEAN
- ARGUE
- COOK
- COMPLAIN
- BE A PEACEMAKER
- IGNORE
- SMILE
- DISOBEY
- PRAY FOR THEM
- FIGHT
- YELL
- BE KIND
- COMPLIMENT
- CRITICIZE
- SPEND TIME TOGETHER
- BE RESPECTFUL

I CAN HELP CARE FOR MY FAMILY

D&C 125-128; VOICES OF THE RESTORATION: BAPTISM FOR OUR ANCESTORS, "A GLORIOUS DOCTRINE"

In D&C 128:5, 12, we learn that all God's children will have the opportunity to be baptized. In the temple, we can baptize those who have died without the ordinance through a proxy baptism. Complete the cross-word puzzle below with words related to this topic.

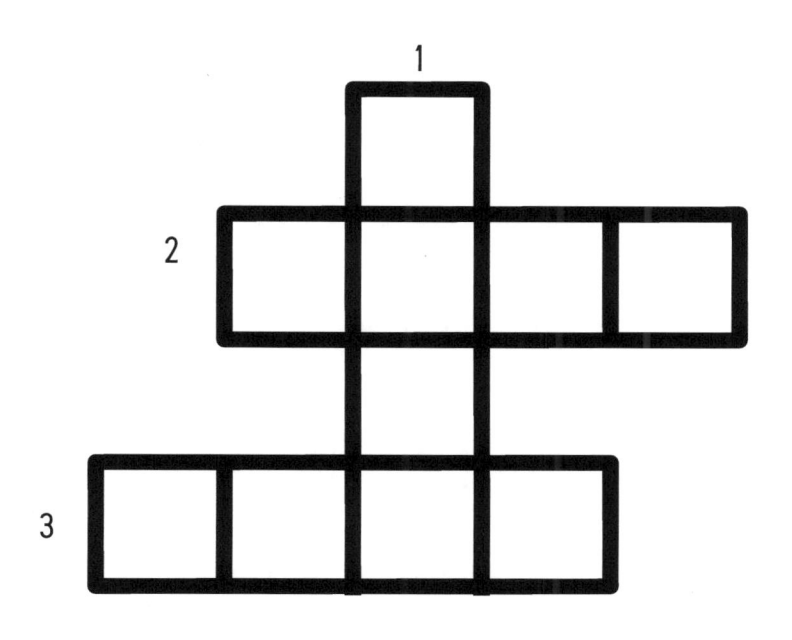

DOWN

1- OUR ANCESTORS WHO WERE NOT BAPTIZED IN THIS _____ NEED US TO DO THEIR ORDINANCES ON THEIR BEHALF.

ACROSS

2- BAPTISMS IN THE TEMPLE ARE PERFORMED FOR THOSE WHO HAVE _____ WITHOUT KNOWLEDGE OF THE GOSPEL.

3- THE TEMPLE BAPTISMAL FONT IS RESTING ON 12 _____

ALL GOD'S CHILDREN SHOULD HAVE THE OPPORTUNITY TO BE BAPTIZED

NOVEMBER 10-16

CIRCLE THE DAYS YOU READ THIS WEEK: MON TUES WED THUR FRI SAT SUN

In D&C 130:22, we learn that Heavenly Father and Jesus Christ have a physical body, but the Holy Ghost does not. Fill in the missing words from these scripture verses. Draw eyes, ears, nose, mouth, and any other details you'd like on the outlines of Heavenly Father and Jesus below.

THE _____ HAS A _____ OF FLESH AND _____ AS TANGIBLE AS MAN'S; THE _____ ALSO; BUT THE HOLY _____ HAS NOT A BODY OF _____ AND BONES, BUT IS A PERSONAGE OF _____ WERE IT NOT SO, THE HOLY GHOST COULD NOT _____ IN US.
-D&C 130:22

SON   GHOST   FATHER   FLESH   BODY   SPIRIT   BONES   DWELL

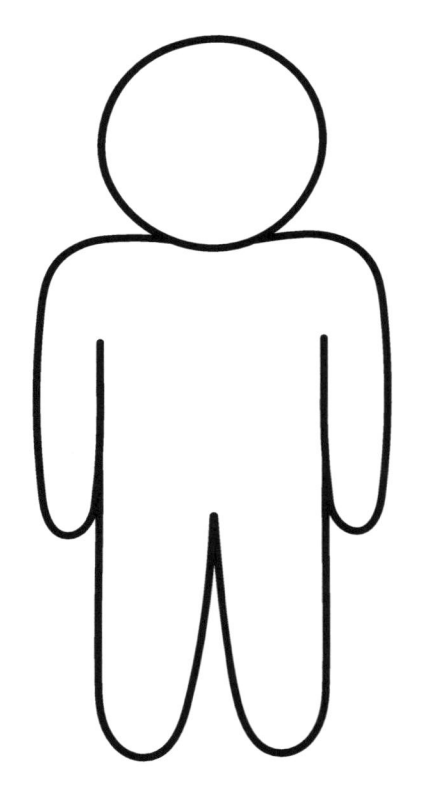

HEAVENLY FATHER & JESUS HAVE AN IMMORTAL PHYSICAL BODY

D&C 129-132

In D&C 132:19, we learn that families can be together for eternity when sealed in the temple. Draw a picture of your family below.

GOD MADE IT POSSIBLE FOR FAMILIES TO BE TOGETHER ETERNALLY

NOVEMBER 17-23

CIRCLE THE DAYS YOU READ THIS WEEK: MON TUES WED THUR FRI SAT SUN

In D&C 133:17-21,25, we read about Jesus coming again. How can you prepare for His Second Coming? Complete the word search below with words related to these verses.

```
I  X  W  O  G  L  P  M  V  Y  N  X  Q  W  V
S  T  N  A  N  E  V  O  C  C  X  I  J  K  H
E  T  N  D  T  P  S  B  K  Y  Q  O  J  N  I
W  D  R  P  P  S  M  L  T  E  P  K  J  X  B
J  S  K  W  B  O  L  A  L  M  G  B  P  K  U
R  W  S  R  J  G  F  A  P  N  H  M  Y  Y  E
R  A  E  G  B  V  L  X  R  D  Y  Z  S  F  A
E  V  R  E  S  C  Y  N  E  I  W  B  U  Q  P
X  W  U  R  P  V  T  X  P  Y  V  U  S  T  X
Q  Q  T  A  H  I  V  H  A  J  I  L  E  H  V
K  U  P  H  W  Y  R  A  R  O  L  N  J  A  U
R  H  I  S  T  E  J  X  E  Y  O  S  Y  N  O
W  D  R  Q  M  O  L  N  H  F  A  M  R  H  A
Q  J  C  P  R  J  I  R  B  U  U  R  I  V  P
L  A  S  R  Q  J  K  Q  D  L  P  U  P  Y  E
```

PREPARE	JESUS	JOYFUL
SCRIPTURES	PRAY	SERVE
SHARE	GOSPEL	COVENANTS

JESUS WILL COME AGAIN

D&C 133-134

In D&C 134:1-2, we read the Lord wants us to obey the law. What would life be like if we didn't have any rules and laws? Match the laws broken with the potential consequences if we didn't have these laws or no one obeyed them.

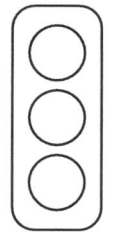

Law Broken	Potential Consequence
NOT STOPPING AT A RED LIGHT	COULD HIT A CHILD & INJURE OR KILL THEM
NOT PAYING FOR ITEMS AT THE STORE	CITIES WOULD BE DANGEROUS IF THERE WERE NO CONSEQUENCE FOR HURTING OTHERS
SPEEDING THROUGH A SCHOOL ZONE	YOU COULD HIT ANOTHER CAR GOING THROUGH THE INTERSECTION
BEATING SOMEONE UP	STORES WOULD GO OUT OF BUSINESS IF NO ONE PAID FOR ITEMS
DRIVING THE WRONG WAY ON A ONE-WAY STREET	COULD HIT ANOTHER VEHICLE HEAD-ON AND CAUSE INJURIES OR DEATH

THE LORD WANTS ME TO OBEY THE LAW

NOVEMBER 24-30

CIRCLE THE DAYS YOU READ THIS WEEK: MON TUES WED THUR FRI SAT SUN

In D&C 135:3, we read of the many great things Joseph Smith did during his life. He and his brother, Hyrum, were murdered in Carthage Jail. On the hearts below, write some of the things Joseph did during his life that have changed your life.

JOSEPH SMITH WAS A PROPHET

D&C 135-136

Shortly after Joseph died, many of the Saints left Nauvoo and went to Winter Quarters to prepare to head west. It was a hard time for the Saints, but the Lord promised to bless them as they stayed faithful (see D&C 136). Color what you'd take with you below. Would you take a handcart or wagon? How many of each item would you need?

THE LORD CAN BLESS ME WHEN I'M STRUGGLING

DECEMBER 1-7

CIRCLE THE DAYS YOU READ THIS WEEK: MON TUES WED THUR FRI SAT SUN

In D&C 138:1-11, we read about what helps us better understand the scriptures. Crack the code to see what we should do.

CRACK THE CODE

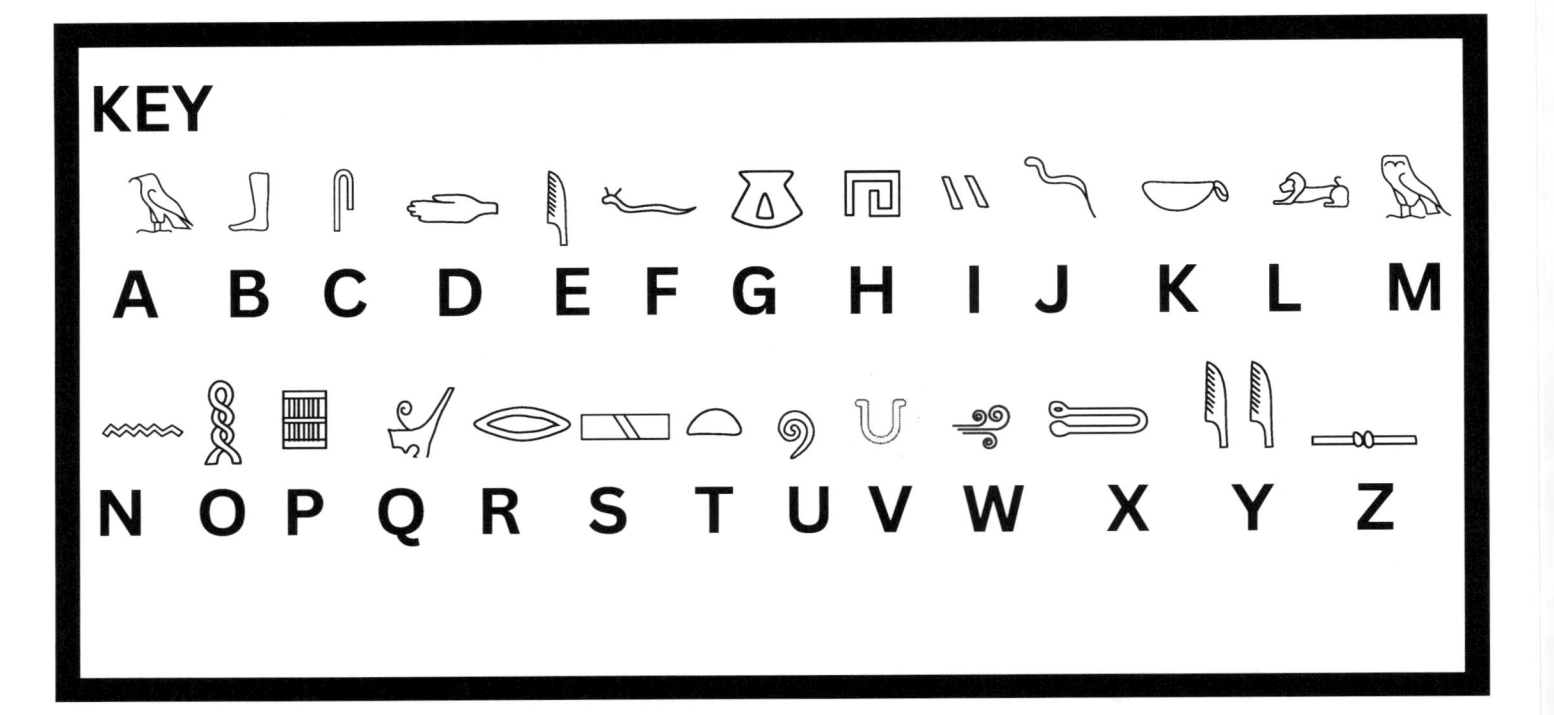

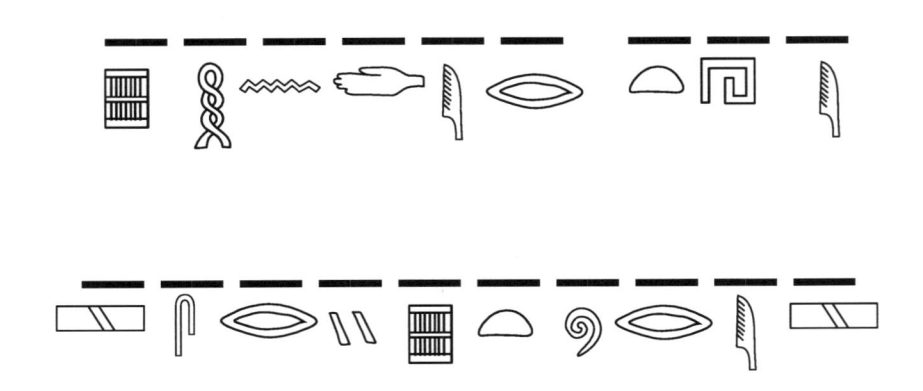

PONDER THE SCRIPTURES

D&C 137-138

In D&C 138:25-60, we read that the Savior's work continues in the Spirit World. Make your way to the center of the maze to find the spirits waiting to be taught the Gospel.

THE SAVIOR'S WORK CONTINUES IN THE SPIRIT WORLD

DECEMBER 8-14

CIRCLE THE DAYS YOU READ THIS WEEK: MON TUES WED THUR FRI SAT SUN

The Articles of Faith explain what The Church of Jesus Christ of Latter-day Saints believes. Write the correct Article of Faith number with it's corresponding summary in the hearts below. Ask your family for help, if needed.

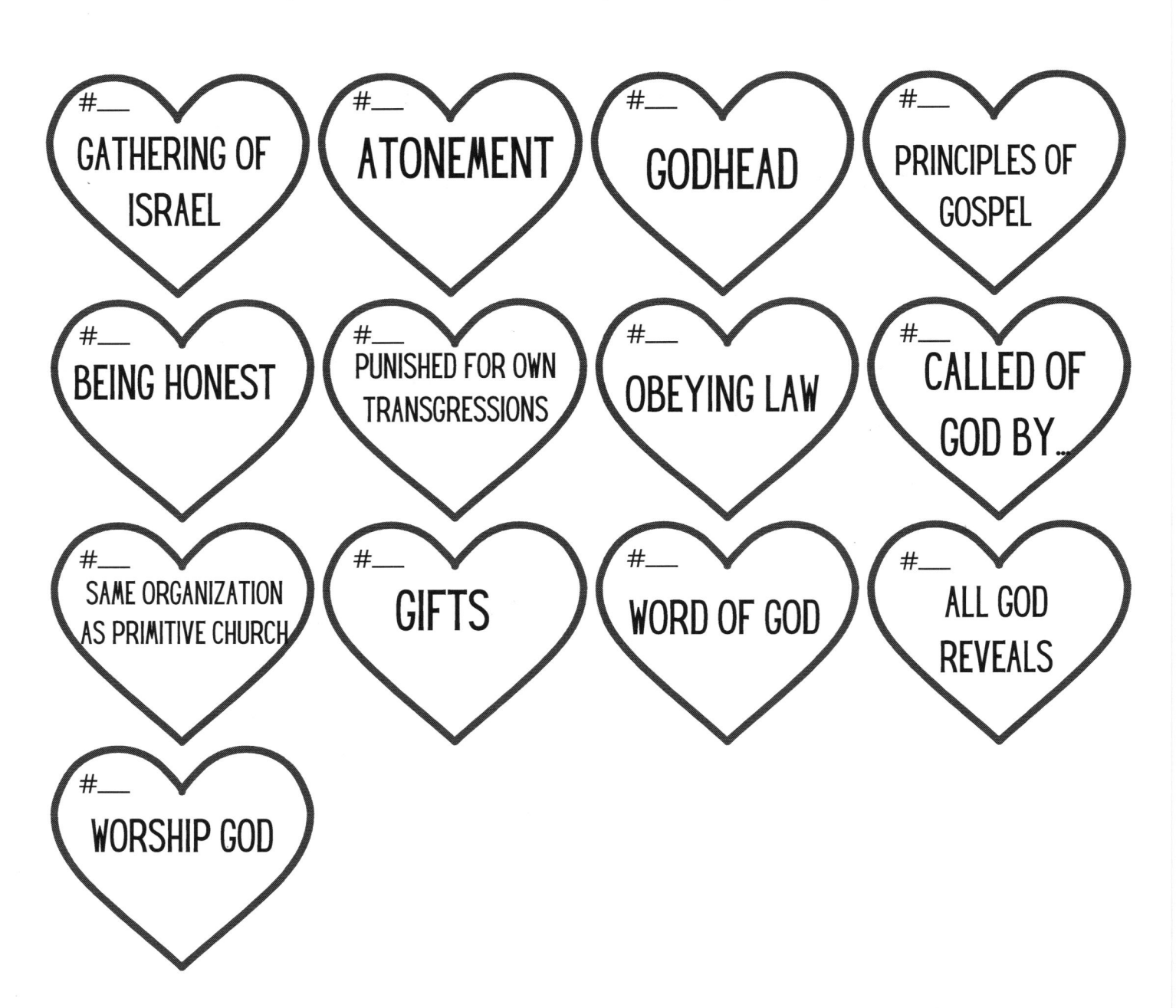

#___ GATHERING OF ISRAEL

#___ ATONEMENT

#___ GODHEAD

#___ PRINCIPLES OF GOSPEL

#___ BEING HONEST

#___ PUNISHED FOR OWN TRANSGRESSIONS

#___ OBEYING LAW

#___ CALLED OF GOD BY...

#___ SAME ORGANIZATION AS PRIMITIVE CHURCH

#___ GIFTS

#___ WORD OF GOD

#___ ALL GOD REVEALS

#___ WORSHIP GOD

I BELIEVE IN JESUS' GOSPEL

THE ARTICLES OF FAITH & OFFICIAL DECLARATIONS 1&2

Official Declaration 2 states that all worthy males may receive God's priesthood, regardless of race. God loves all of His children. How many words can you make from the letters in "God loves all His children"?

GOD LOVES ALL HIS CHILDREN

GOD LOVES ALL OF HIS CHILDREN

DECEMBER 15-21

CIRCLE THE DAYS YOU READ THIS WEEK: MON TUES WED THUR FRI SAT SUN

We learn about the importance of families in "The Family: A Proclamation to the World". Color the picture of the family below.

FAMILIES ARE IMPORTANT IN HEAVENLY FATHER'S PLAN

THE FAMILY: A PROCLAMATION TO THE WORLD

In "The Family Proclamation", we learn that successful families are built upon certain principles. These principles can be found in the word search below.

```
O A C N D K W O J Q U O F Q U
H T I A F O B Z M S F O D P U
Q K N T R X S Q L U R L A H H
I J B K L S M D S G Q Q R U R
S U N O M P O Q I X J R A N D
V H V N S Z R V V F F U A M L
F E V M P I E P S Y S X K R X
A K W Q P N Y O N B C S A I B
L U S L E I A E R Y E L W A L
F B Y S A W R G P E T E R Z V
J H S A D M P N U F S A L W M
Z F T E G N O I S S A P M O C
D F N O I T A E R C E R E S C
K O E R L G K H S P O B N C C
S I E C N A T N E P E R F X T
```

FAITH	PRAYER	REPENTANCE
FORGIVENESS	RESPECT	LOVE
COMPASSION	WORK	RECREATION

FAMILIES ARE HAPPIEST WHEN THEY FOLLOW JESUS

DECEMBER 22-28

CIRCLE THE DAYS YOU READ THIS WEEK: MON TUES WED THUR FRI SAT SUN

In the second paragraph of the "Living Christ," we see some of the many good things Jesus went about doing. How can you serve others like He did? Color the picture below.

JESUS WENT ABOUT DOING GOOD

CHRISTMAS

Think of the many blessings and gifts you have in your life because of Jesus. Write or draw those items in the gift boxes below.

JESUS CHRIST HAS GIVEN ME MANY GIFTS

GOAL REFLECTION

How did you do with your spiritual, physical, social, and intellectual goals the past year? Discuss with your family. In space below, write or draw a picture of something you have learned from studying the Doctrine and Covenants this year.

★★★★★

IF YOU ENJOYED THIS BOOK, MAKE SURE TO LEAVE A REVIEW.

CHECK OUT OUR OTHER BOOKS.

FOLLOW US ONLINE!

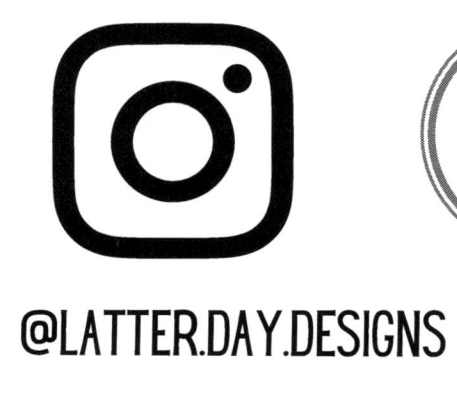

@LATTER.DAY.DESIGNS

LATTER-DAY DESIGNS

Made in United States
Troutdale, OR
03/10/2025